HYPNOSIS

Powerful And Fast Working Hypnosis Techniques To Hypnotize Anyone Now !

L. Jordan

3rd EDITION

Free gift inside this book

© 2016 Copyright.

Text copyright reserved. L. Jordan

The contents of this book may not be reproduced, duplicated or transmitted without direct written permission from the author

Disclaimer : All attempts have been made by the author to provide factual and accurate content. No responsibility will be taken by the author for any damages caused by misuse of the content described in this book. The content of this book has been derived from various sources. Please consult a licensed professional before attempting any techniques outlined in this book.

Table of Contents

Introduction 4

Chapter 1: Introduction To Hypnosis 5

Chapter 2: How Can Hypnosis Help? 18

Chapter 3: How To Do Hypnosis 23

Chapter 4: The Scope of Covert Hypnosis 28

Chapter 5: Implementation of Conversational Hypnosis...... 33

Chapter 6: How the Hypnotic Gaze Works 38

Chapter 7: How To Influence Emotions During Hypnosis ... 46

Chapter 8: How To Discharge Emotional Baggage by Self Hypnosis.. 50

Chapter 9: How to Hypnotize a Friend................................... 57

Chapter 10: Instant Hypnosis 63

Chapter 11: Self-Hypnosis Method 68

Chapter 12: How To Tell That Someone Is In A Trance......... 79

Chapter 13: Major Mistakes To Avoid In Hypnosis 84

Conclusion.. 90

Bonus.. 91

Introduction

What is hypnosis really? When you say hypnosis in a room, most people are going to conjure up the image of a stadium of people watching as those on stage do a variety of amusing things. These people may be walking like a crab, or talking like a chicken all of this while the hypnotist stands and makes various sounds or says key trigger words to get them to do these things. Whether this is a sham or these people really are under a "spell" is not the question what is, the question is, is that what hypnosis really is?

The simple answer is no. While it is a form of hypnosis and some of it may be real and some of it may not it is not truly what hypnosis is. Hypnosis is a suggestive tool that when done right can help people immensely. When you know how to hypnotize someone you can help them to stop smoking, find pain relief and a variety of other things. More than that once you have mastered the powerful hypnosis techniques required to actually do some good you can even hypnotize yourself and encourage your own better behavior through this suggestion.

Chapter 1:
Introduction To Hypnosis

When you Google hypnosis you will come up with a variety of meanings for this powerful tool. It is perhaps the APA also known as the American Psychological Association describes hypnosis as team interplay where a participant or patient behaves in accordance with the suggestions of the hypnotist. Thanks to the popular stage acts where people are provoked to perform funny or unusual actions, hypnosis has garnered a well-known reputation and is often associated with a negative light. Hypnosis has however been proven in a clinical setting to provide many benefits both medicinal and therapeutic benefits, the most common worked with is reducing pain and nervousness. There are some camps who even suggest that, with the proper technique, hypnosis may even help patients who have the beginning signs of dementia. When you look at it in that light Hypnosis becomes a powerful tool that you can use to help your friends and loved ones.

If you are thinking about swinging a watch back and forth while saying you are getting sleepy very sleepy, as popular media would have you think, you have to adjust your thinking. The process of truly hypnotizing someone is very different than what is commonly pictured. When you truly hypnotize someone you encourage them into a state of trance that can be like sleep, some who have been hypnotized often describe the experience as a state of focused attention in which the person who is put under is more suggestible and can have vivid fantasy visions.

What Is Hypnosis?

The idea of hypnosis has been discussed for a few hundred years, but science is still not able to explain how hypnosis actually works. It's obvious what a person does under hypnosis, but it's not clear as to why they do it. This little puzzle piece is actually a piece in a much larger puzzle of how the human mind operates, but it's unlikely that scientists are going to arrive at an explanation of this phenomena in our foreseeable future, so hypnosis is most likely going to remain a mystery, too.

However, psychiatrists do understand the overall symptoms displayed when someone is under hypnosis, so they do have an idea of how it works. Hypnosis is a trance that is characterized by relaxation, suggestibility, and heightened imagination. The person who is under hypnosis is alert the entire time, but they appear to be asleep most often. Hypnosis is usually compared to the act of daydreaming, or the feeling of losing yourself in a movie or a book. You're conscious, but you've tuned out the stimuli around you in everyday life. You are focused mentally on the subject in front of you and excluding almost any other thought process.

When you're in an everyday trance, such as watching a movie or daydreaming, the imaginary world is real to you in the sense that it engages your emotions. Events that we imagine can cause us real sadness, fear, or happiness, and you could jolt in your seat if you're surprised. Some researchers categorize this as self-hypnosis. Most psychiatrists emphasize on the trance state that's brought on by deliberate relaxation and concentration. This hypnosis that is deep is compared to a relaxed mental state between being awake and asleep.

Early History

Meditation is actually a form of hypnosis, so the practice of it has been around for thousands upon thousands of years. However, the scientific concept of this practice did not originate until the late 1700's. Franz Mesmer was actually the father of hypnotism. He was an Austrian physician who believed that hypnosis was a mystical force that flowed from the hypnotist to the patient. He labeled this phenomenon animal magnetism.

Critics were quick to dismiss the magical element of his practice, especially the part where he believed that the hypnotist has a sort of power over the patient. The practice of hypnotism was actually known as mesmerizing, named after Mesmer, and we still use the term mesmerize today.

In the old-school style of hypnotism, you approach the suggestions of the person hypnotizing you or your own ideas as if they were actually reality. If the hypnotist has suggested that the patient's tongue has swollen to twice its normal size, the patient is going to feel that sensation in their mouth and have trouble talking. If they suggest that the patient is drinking a strawberry milkshake, that person is going to taste the milkshake and feel it as it cools the throat and mouth. If they suggest that someone is afraid, they are going to feel fear. The entire time, the patient is aware that everything is fake. Essentially, they are playing pretend like kids do, but on a more intense level.

In this mental state, the patient feels relaxed and uninhibited. That's because they tune out the worries and doubts that normally control their actions and thoughts. They may experience the same feeling as they're watching a movie. They're so engrossed in what's happening that their worries about their family, job, and personal life just fade away. Then they're just thinking about what's happening on the screen.

In a state of hypnotism, the patient is highly suggestible. When the hypnotist informs the patient to do something, the patient will most likely embrace that idea and do it. This is what makes a stage hypnotist so entertaining. Normally sensible, reserved adults will walk around the stage acting like a chicken or singing at the top of their lungs. Embarrassment seems to fly out the window and the patient's sense of safety is gone. A hypnotist cannot get the patient to do something they do not want to do, however.

So what is behind all of this?

Hypnotism Revealed

The main theory of hypnosis is that it's a way to open up a person's subconscious mind. Normally, we're aware of the thought processes of our conscious mind, such as the problems that you have to solve, the words you speak, and maybe where you left your keys.

However, the conscious mind is actually working directly with the subconscious mind, or the mind that is 'behind the scenes'. The subconscious mind is able to access the reservoir of information that allows you to solve a problem, speak a coherent sentence, or locate those pesky keys. It creates a plan and ideas and converses with your conscious mind. When a new idea pops into your mind out of the blue, it's because the subconscious mind was working on solving a problem for you and it believes it found a solution. It's up to your conscious mind to determine if that solution is good or not.

The subconscious mind also takes care of all those things you do that are automatic, such as breathing. You don't actively have to think about taking a breath and releasing it. The subconscious mind controls that function. You don't think about all the little moves you make to drive a car, or ride a bike, because all those small things that lead to driving the car or riding the bike are taken care of by the subconscious. The subconscious processes the physical info that the body receives.

So really, the subconscious mind is the brains behind the operation. It actually does most of your thinking and decides a lot about what you do in your everyday life. When you're awake, the conscious mind evaluates those thoughts and makes decisions about them. It will process the new information and relay that information to the subconscious mind. However, when you're sleeping, the conscious mind is out of the way and the subconscious mind is the only one present.

Psychiatrists believe that the deep focusing and relaxation of hypnotism subdue and calm your conscious mind so that it's taking a less active approach in your thinking behavior. In a state of hypnosis, you are aware of what is happening, but your conscious mind has taken the backseat and is allowing the subconscious mind to drive. This allows the hypnotist to work directly with that subconscious mind and bypass the conscious one. Hypnotism sort of opens up the control panel of your brain.

In many studies, researchers have compared the physical signs of hypnotic subjects to those who are not hypnotized. In most of the studies, they found that there was not a significant physical change that was associated with the state of hypnosis.

The subject's respiration and heart rate slowed, but that was due to relaxation and not the hypnotic state itself.

There have been appearances of changes in the activity of the brain, though. The most notable research comes from electroencephalography or EEGs. These are the measurement of the electrical activity going on in the brain. Extensive research in this field has shown that the brain produces different brain waves and rhythms depending on its mental state. Deep sleep has a different brain wave pattern than those who are dreaming.

In some cases, there were EEG readings that showed patients under hypnosis had a boost in the lower frequency waves that are common in dreaming and sleep, and they had a drop in the higher frequency ones that are common to being fully awake. Brain-wave information is not a conclusive indicator of how the method of hypnosis works, but the pattern does fit the hypothesis that the conscious mind is not really present during hypnosis and that the subconscious mind is the one that is in control.

Researchers have also looked at the patterns in the cerebral cortex that happen when someone is hypnotized. In these findings, hypnotic patients showed a reduce activity level in the left hemisphere of the cortex. This is your logical control center or the part of the brain that deducts and reasons. Activity in the right hemisphere was shown to increase. A decrease in the left part of the brain points toward hypnosis subduing the mind's inhibitions. And at the same time, an increase in the activity of the right side of the brain supports that idea that the impulsive, creative subconscious has taken over. This isn't conclusive, but it does lend support to the idea that hypnotism uses the subconscious mind.

Whether or not hypnosis is a physiological occurrence, millions of people practice it on a regular basis, and millions of people have reported that it worked.

Hypnosis Methods

The different methods of hypnosis may vary, but they all have a few basic rules:

- The patient has to want to be hypnotized.
- The patient has to believe they can actually be hypnotized.
- The patient must feel comfortable and relaxed during the hypnosis.

If all of these criteria are met, then the hypnotist can guide their patient into a trance using a few different methods. The most common of those methods include the following:

Fixed-Gaze Induction
Also known as eye fixation, this method is the one that is often seen played out in movies or on a stage. The hypnotist will wave a pocket watch or another form of object on a string in front of their patient. The basic idea of this form of hypnotism is to get the person to focus on that object so intently that they forget about everything around them. All that external stimuli is blocked out. As the person focuses, the hypnotist will speak to them in a low voice and lull them into feeling relaxed. This method was popular in the early days, but it's not used as much today because it doesn't work with most of the population.

Rapid
This method of hypnotism is meant to overload the person's mind with some sudden, firm commands. If the commands are powerful enough and the hypnotist is believable, then the person will surrender their conscious ability to control the situation. This method will work well for a stage hypnotist because the circumstances of being up in front of the audience already has the person on edge, and this makes them more susceptible to the hypnotist's commands.

Imagery and Progressive Relaxation
If you've ever lain down and tried the meditation technique of relaxing your entire body, you've put yourself into a state where you could potentially be hypnotized. This method is very commonly used by psychiatrists. By speaking to the person in a slow, soothing tone, the hypnotist is able to gradually bring on relaxation and focus to the person. This eases them into full hypnosis. Typically, self-hypnosis exercises, meditation, and audio tapes use this progressive relaxation method.

Loss of Balance
The main part of this method is the slow, rhythmic rocking of the person being hypnotized. Parents have been using this method for thousands of years to put their babies to sleep.

Before hypnotists bring their subject into a trance, they generally test the willingness of their subject and their capacity to be hypnotized. The typical testing method is to use a few different statements. These statements include:

- Relax your arms completely

- Pretend you are weightless

These suggestions get more outrageous because the hypnotist is attempting to get the person to suspend their belief for the time being.

Depending on that person's personality and mental state, the entire process can take anywhere from a few minutes to half an hour. Hypnotists see this odd mental state a powerful tool with many different possibilities.

What is the effect of hypnosis?

Every person is going to have a very different experience under hypnosis. One person may report a feeling of supreme separation or supreme relaxation during the process while another may say that they feel their actions appear to be occurring outside of their conscious and beyond their control. Still yet other people will report that while under hypnosis they remain awake and in a full state of awareness and are able to carry out full conversations during the process.

There have been experiments performed by renowned researcher Ernest Hilgard that have demonstrated how hypnosis can be acclimated to dramatically alter perceptions. After an individual who was under hypnosis was authoritatively mandated not to feel pain in his or her arm the person's arm was placed in freezing water. While those in the test group who were not hypnotized had to absent their arm after just a few seconds due to the amount of pain caused those who had been placed in hypnosis and authoritatively mandated not to feel the pain were able to leave their arm in the cold liquid for minutes without feeling any pain.

What Can Hypnosis Be Used For?

While in a later chapter we will cover the broad range of things that hypnosis can be applied to we will begin with a simple list of just some of them to show you the full range of what hypnotism can do:

- The treatment of long-term pain conditions such as rheumatoid arthritis.

- The treatment control of the pain brought on by having a child.

- The treatment in reducing the symptoms of dementia

- Hypnotherapy may be able to reduce some symptoms of ADHD.

- The reduction of vomiting in patients who have cancer and must be treated with radiation and chemotherapy.

- Control of pain during a trip to the dentist

- Control of the pain and side effects of skin conditions that include warts and psoriasis.

- Reducing the painful symptoms that can go with IBS (irritable bowel syndrome)

Will it work for you?

There are many people who think that they can't be hypnotized, they think they are too strong of mind or that it is all a bunch of fake trances. However, research has shown that a larger number of people are able to be put into a hypnotic state than they think. The research shows:

Up to 15% of people in the world will respond to being hypnotized.

Children are more often easier to put under hypnosis than adults are.

There are about 10% of the adult population that are unable to or very difficult to put under hypnosis.

Those who are easily absorbed in stories of fantasy are much more likely to be hypnotized than those who are not.

If you are interested in being hypnotized, you must remember to approach the experience and process with an open mind. Once again, research has shown that those who go into it with an open mind and a willingness, as well as a positive outlook, are more likely to respond to the process.

Theories and myths

There are several theories of hypnosis, but one of the best recognized is called, Hilgard's no dissociation theory of hypnosis. According to Hilgard, those people who are in a hypnotic state will experience a split consciousness. During this split, there are two different streams of noetic activity, one stream of consciousness responds to the hypnotist's suggestions. Meanwhile, another dissociated stream processes information outside of the hypnotized individual's conscious vigilance.

Along with theories as with anything that is in the mainstream, but not considered typical medical treatment there are myths.

<u>Myth 1</u>: Upon waking up from a session of hypnosis you won't remember anything that happened while under.

While there are rare cases of amnesia happening to those who have been put under hypnosis it is more common that the subject will remember everything that occurred while being hypnotized. That said, however, hypnosis can have a large effect on memory. Posthypnotic amnesia is something that can rarely occur causing a subject to forget what happened while they were under hypnosis. This effect is however usually found to be limited and temporary, lasting at most a day or two.

<u>Myth 2</u>: Hypnosis can enhance memory of events such as criminal events that were witnessed.

While it is true that hypnosis can be acclimated to avail enhance recollection the effects of this have been inordinately glamorized in popular media. There has been research done which has found that hypnosis does not lead to greater recollection enhancement or precision. In fact, it has been proven that hypnosis can lead to mendacious or distorted recollections so it is best not to be utilized in criminal investigations.

<u>Myth 3</u>: It is possible to be hypnotized even if you don't want to be.

Once again the media have been strong in suggesting that you can be hypnotized whether you want to be or not. The truth is, however, that to actually be hypnotized you must voluntarily participate in the process and you can't be forced into it.

Myth 4: The hypnotist is able to control all of your actions while you are under hypnosis.

It can often seem thatwhileunder hypnosis, you are doing things against your will that is not the case. The hypnotist will influence and guide you towards your goal, but they cannot make you perform actions that are against your values or morals.

Myth 5: Hypnosis can make you stronger, faster and just in general better at sports.

While there are forms of hypnosis that can help to enhance performance it cannot actually make you stronger or more athletic beyond what you can physically handle. It tends to take away the mental blocks of limitation in order to help you do better.

Chapter 2:
How Can Hypnosis Help?

A short bit of research on hypnosis will show you that it is most commonly used for weight control or as a tool to stop smoking today. While it can effectively be used for both of these, hypnosis can also be used for a variety of other issues and daily activities. Hypnosis can be very effective when you work with problems such as specific phobias (fears), pain management, empowerment, grief resolution, stress and relaxation, motivation, confidence issues, self-esteem, and academic enhancement. With the right tools and the right powerful hypnosis technique, you can help anyone with the power of hypnosis.

Can Hypnosis help you control your weight?

One of the top uses of hypnosis today is helping the battle of the bulge. When many of us step on a scale, we deal with frustration and even anger at what we see, especially if we are already doing a diet and workout regime. Often times we think "I have eaten what I should, done what I should why am I not losing weight?!"

The fact is the goal may be achieved but when we burn fat in our bodies, nature builds lean muscle. From there our body goes on to build stronger and better bone as well. Fat takes up more space in your bodies, however, lean muscle and bone will weigh more than fat. It is better if we focus more on the way our clothing is fitting then the pounds that the scale is showing.

The first challenge you have when going into any kind of weight loss is to change the perspective of what you will be doing. You must change your idea of what you are seeing when you step on the scale.

Weight Loss has a lot of negative emotion connected with it. When you hear someone say weight loss, you tend to associate a deep struggle, being unhappy and being hungry all he time with it. Also, the simple fact is when we as people lose something our first instinct is to find it again. While we may want to lose the weight, something inside of us might tell us to find it again. Instead, use a different term, slimming down or toning up so that it is not such a negative wording.

Everyone on the planet is on one kind of diet or another. Everything that you eat or drink is a form of diet whether it is good or bad. It is Garfield who pointed out perfectly as well when looking at the word diet, it is just die with a T on the end of it. Rather than looking at it in a negative way of dieting, look at it in terms of life change. That change is changing how you eat and what you eat.

As previously mentioned the focus should be less on the pounds that the scale says and more about the clothing fit. Focus on a goal size that you would like to be and once you have achieved your goal, celebrate no matter how much the scale says you weigh.

Those who work with weight control in hypnosis believe that how you view yourself is an important part of a weight loss program when hypnosis is involved. The image that one holds in their mind tends to be the image that the body will emulate. If you have a view of yourself as being a fat person, your body will continue to stay that way. Through the process of hypnotherapy and hypnosis, an old image of yourself is replaced when you picture and create a new picture of yourself, one that you can relate to more and feel comfortable.

This new image of a healthy and fit you is an image that the body will now conform to. Also, the hypnotist will provide suggestions to increase the drive for you to drink water and decrease the drive to eat foods that are high in fat and create a desire for a healthy lifestyle. This, therefore, will work with how and when you eat as well as why you're eating and the emotions that come with eating.

How does hypnosis work to stop smoking?

Most smokers started when they were young for a variety of reasons, peer pressure, simple teenage rebellion or because it was what everyone around them was doing at the time. When you use hypnosis to help cure smoking, you will take the person you are working with back to revisit those events with the view of the adult they are now. Make them see through the hypnosis that the harmful behavior they are doing today was simply the rebellion of their younger selves. With that addressed you will also want to tell your subject suggested things to do instead of smoke when they have a craving, chew gum, exercise make them focus on anything but smoking.

Can hypnosis help a long time phobia?

The simple answer is yes it can. No matter how long someone has suffered from a specific phobia, the power of hypnosis can help no matter when the phobia began to affect your daily life. The only requirement is that the subject truly wishes to change and goes into the process with an open mind.

Like with other habits, the origins of phobias usually start in the innocence of childhood usually something happens that sets off the issue. More often than not it is not something actually traumatic but a small incident. During the hypnosis session, the subject will revisit that incident with the viewpoint of an adult. It is through this process that the adult can see that what happened was harmless and from there they can change their larger memory of the problem. Once the memory has been changed it will remove the phobia that has long been associated with this incident.

What kind of pain is hypnosis able to help you with?

Pain is often seen as a villain and truly as much as it is not a fun thing it is not a villain. Pain is the body's way of saying there is something wrong with me or you need to slow down and let me catch up. The problem for most people is when the receptors in the body used to alert to pain start to alert and work overtime. The subconscious part of the brain is something that can be used as a great tool for pain removal of any kind. This tool can take care of the pain that has been caused by daily headaches, jitters before surgery, pain after surgery and many more. One single hypnosis session can create a sense of well-being in a person that is enough to chase the pain away.

I have a great deal of stress and drama in my life, can hypnosis help with that?

In today's world, we find ourselves living in a busy world that can sometimes seem to be a hurry up and wait life. We have obligations upon obligations, those of family, work, and even events that are supposed to be fun. We are often pulled in many directions at once and the body naturally reacts to that. The body reacts by getting tense. This can cause headaches, joint pain, and a feeling of overwhelming urges. There have been documented cases that parents hitting other parents or road rage stems from a schedule that has been too busy.

It is through the power of hypnosis that the body can learn how to let all of this go and relax. With the right techniques, a single word or thought can be used to trigger the high level of total relaxation at any time. Being able to relax like this will help your overall health. Hypnosis can't change the number of items on your daily schedule, but it can help manage reactions to them better.

I can't get over the death of a loved one. I feel like I will never feel right or happy again. Can hypnosis help?

Even when someone has been sick for a long time and death is expected, we as humans are never fully prepared for it. A sudden death is even worse and both kinds of death leave survivors with unresolved issues, guilt or anger that can seem to never go away, they can seem as if one will never be the same again.

Hypnosis is a good way to let out feelings and resolve them in a healthy and safe way where no one including the one grieving is harmed. Hypnosis as a tool can be used to overcome the feelings of anger, guilt and even betrayal that one may feel after someone dies.

In short there are very few limits as to what hypnosis can help with. It is a powerful tool and all you have to do is apply the correct technique to help anyone with their issues. The next chapters of this book will teach you the most powerful techniques of hypnosis so you can put anyone under.

Chapter 3:
How To Do Hypnosis

There are several ways to hypnotize someone the first and most common way is professionally called the progressive relaxation technique. This is the type of hypnotism that you most commonly see on television, in the movies or being displayed at very fairs and festivals across the United States It is easy to do and powerful enough to put anyone under.

Ensure that your subject is comfortable. Have them lie down or sit in a way that will be comfortable for any period of time that you need them to. Also, make sure that you as the hypnotist are comfortable. Ensure that the room or location you choose for this process has little to no distraction in it.

Step 1: Induction

The process of induction is the core process of what you do as a hypnotist. It sets the stage and gets the subject into the trance state you need them in to then offer your suggestions. Once your subject is comfortable and you are as well begin the process by having them close their eyes and imagine themselves in a happy place. As you speak to them, use a modulated steady tone with an even pace. Tell them this happy place should be where they feel safe, and secure. It can be a meadow with a gently bubbling stream, or laying on the beach listening to the ocean. As you talk to them elaborate that this place should make them feel calm, get them to focus on the calming aspects of their happy place. Ensure as you work on this segment that they won't laugh or become distracted by their happy place as you need them to focus on being calm.

Continue to speak in your low modulated voice and pace it with the subjects breathing as they relax more. You will continue to repeat similar phrases about their happy place and how calm they need to be. This repetition can bore the conscious brain and start to encourage it to take a back seat so you can access the subconscious.

As your subjects breathing becomes more even begin to ask them to relax their entire body. Using terms such as, "Let your feet relax, now let your legs, then your hips and waist relax. Feel any tension in your chest, leaving, let your chest, relax now your arms. Feel your shoulders relax and your neck. Feel it as your entire body begins to relax into a place where you feel peaceful. You should feel no stress nothing at all." Continue this simple process with a firm but modulated tone over and over again until you are sure it is working on your subject.

As your subject's body relaxes ask them to feel themselves flying through the atmosphere. Utilizing your modulated tone forcefully (but calmly) authorize them to feel the wind through their hair and to picture themselves laughing with the bliss of the feeling. Tell them there is no stress, no worries, no cares. Forcefully authorize them to then land on a cloud and feel the softness of that cloud. Then they are required to envision themselves sinking down into the cloud. The more that they sink down into the cloud into the softness there is more relaxation, worries will flow away like a river, going until gone. Utilizing the same modulated tone the entire time instructively authorize them to visualize all of your stress and all of your worries and cares flowing out every last one of them should go down that flowing river. and instructively authorize them to feel those feelings should be superseded by relaxation.

As they fall more into relaxation, you will keep the same tone and start to change your instructions to your subject and begin to make suggestions. These suggestions need to be designed to increase the feeling of relaxation and the strength of it overall. Tell them suggestions such as, "With the stress and worries gone you can feel yourself relaxed now. Your body feels almost heavy with the relaxation. The more I talk to you the more you will feel heavy and deeply relaxed. Let this feeling wash you into a deep and peaceful place, a peaceful state of hypnosis."

Now you will begin to use your subjects general body language and their breathing as a guide for you. It is important when you use hypnosis to be good at reading body language. Use their body language as a guide and repeat suggestions as needed. Repeat them several times all in the same tone you have been using. Repeat them until you are sure they are totally relaxed. Examples of the phrases you can use for this repetition include:

"Every word that I say to you is putting you faster into a state of hypnosis. You will be buried into hypnosis, faster and farther so that you will stay rooted inside the hypnosis."

"Sink down and shut down. Sink down and shut down. Sink down and shut down until you are shutting down fully."

"The farther in you go, the deeper you are able to go. The deeper you go, the farther you want to go, and the farther you go, the more relaxed you feel, the more you enjoy it."

Once you feel that your subject is in a completely relaxed trance, you will want to gently conclude the induction. You can do it with a phrase such as "Now you are resting and comfortable in a deep, restful sleep. You are going deeper and faster and deeper and faster into that sleep the whole time until I bring you back. While you rest, you will only have to take in and accept the suggestions that help you. The suggestions that you are willing to take in and willing to do. You will never have to accept any suggestion that is not for your benefit or anything that you are not willing to accept. The choice is yours."

Step 2: During hypnosis the suggestions

Once your subject is fully under your control, you will want to give them the powerful positive suggestions that will help them achieve the goal that they came to you for. Do not try to scare them into a new way of being, this tactic does not work and could possibly undo the hypnotic work you have done to get them into atrance. Focus on positive terms and phrases to guide them into the goal range.

Step 3: End the session

This is perhaps the easiest part of the process as you will basically just be asking your subject to come back and stop picturing things. You can use this time not only to bring them back, but get in one last good positive suggestion for them.

Begin bringing them back by using a statement such as, " I will now count down starting with the number five. By the time I get to the number one, you will wake up. You will feel well rested like a full night sleep and wide awake. Better than a cup of coffee." Before you start the count this is where you can insert that final positive phrase such as "as a result of this experience you are going to find and feel fantastic changes in your life." or a comment more personally geared to what you had hypnotized them for. Then you simply do your countdown and the session is complete.

Chapter 4:
The Scope of Covert Hypnosis

When does hypnosis become covert? Well, when you exercise covert hypnosis, you are simply trying to get into contact with someone else' mind without them knowing that you are working at it. In fact, it often happens in what appears to be normal conversation. So do not get surprised to hear covert hypnosis being referred to as conversational hypnosis. Although you need to learn and practice covert hypnosis in detail, it will help for you to learn first what it entails.

The most common techniques of covert hypnosis:

Using eye cues
Eye cues are part of the process of reading and comprehending someone's body language. Just by observing a person's body language, it is possible to tell what a person is thinking. You get a good idea what images they are forming, the nature of the sounds they are registering, and generally how they are feeling.

Even better, when you look into someone's eyes, you get a good idea what their thought process is. If you are keen, you can even tell whether they are actually thinking something or they are remembering it. Of paramount importance is the movement of the person's eyes. The eye movements can give you a good idea what the person is in the process of assessing. Of course, the using eye cues for successful hypnosis is a skill that takes some patience to master, but it is actually effective.

Applying sub-modalities
In the technique of sub-modalities, you kind of experiment with select words, observing which of those triggers some form of response from the person you are trying to hypnotize. Certain words will evoke eye cues; others will affect the person's body language; others the voice tone; and so on. Some of those responses will be positive while others negative.

The strength in covert hypnotism lies in your keen observation because you need to keep repeating the words that you notice invoke the response you want. Of course the person's physical response or eye cues are indication of what their thought process is.

Using a form of Deception
Deception in hypnotism involves using language that makes the other person trust your suggestion of what the reality is; making them relax and letting you into their thought process. The language that ends up helping you in hypnotism sometimes conveys false information. However, it does work in creating rapport between you and the person you are trying to hypnotize.

Using Misdirection
This technique involves you using suggestions in different contexts than would bring out the truth; and that is in a bid to confuse the person into accepting your suggestion. And you do it in a manner that leaves little room for the person to analyze exactly what you said in its current context vis -a-vis what it would mean in a different context.

In fact you can equate this deception with the one that magicians do, only that magician's divert your attention to something else while they do an act that they did not want you to notice. It is actually a way of suggesting some truth when you know it is false, but knowing quite well that if you make a direct suggestion the other person will call you out as a liar.

Applying Cold Reading

In cold reading, what you do is make the person you are trying to hypnotize believe that you can really read their mind. So you observe them keenly without making it obvious that you are trying to assess them, and you learn whatever you can from their demeanor. From what you deduce from your observation you can then formulate a statement, with the intention of making that person believe you can see right through them and know what kind of person they are.

And the kind of statement that you make needs to be general so that no part of it can be nailed as untrue. For instance, instead of telling someone that they are definitely shy, you could make a statement that provokes an affirmation or one that provokes the person into volunteering more insightful information. You could, for instance, say:

I have this feeling that sometimes you have no reservations in expressing yourself, yet you sometimes find yourself reflecting on the past.

Now, this kind of statement can evoke a range of responses from the person you have just addressed, and so you need to listen carefully to their response in order to understand where they stand with their feelings. What they tell you is what you ride on to further your hypnosis. The person might tell you in response to your statement:

Sure, I am expressive but also reflective

I have a tendency to reflect and not express

Oh, yes

Well, sort of

Notice that while the person has not said you are wrong, their response is not very informative. However, whatever response you get has some pointer that you can pursue to attract more information. So you use that response to design another general statement to pose to that person; a follow up statement. And from that you can get information that can help you understand the person almost to the point of exactness. Of course, after the first two general statements you will be in a position to ask questions of a more direct nature without feeling awkward or intrusive.

Applying Warm Reading
You apply warm reading by stating things that cannot be disputed. And the reason what you state cannot be disputed is not because you have learnt a lot about the person you are seeking to hypnotize, but because the statement is so general that something about it must be true. In essence, warm reading is more general than cold reading because in cold reading you have some observation to go by while in warm reading, you just wittily design a believable statement. Look at warm reading more like an ice breaker than a display of knowledge.

Here is an example of a warm reading statement:

It seems you have had different experiences in your life. I can also see that some of those experiences have influenced your understanding of the people around you.

Look – life is about experiences; that is, varying experiences. And that applies to everyone. Nobody has one uniform experience in life in all circumstances. So, yes – the statement cannot be faulted even when you hardly know this person you are talking about. Yet, the person gets to believe, as is human nature, that the statement you made was particularly unique to them. The impact of this...? The person gets to respond genuinely and you get to learn about them easily as they react spontaneously to your facts.

Applying hot reading
In hot reading, the information you provide the person you are trying to hypnotize is spot on. Does that mean that hot reading is only performed by psychics? Well, yes... um, no. I mean, in the eyes of your subject of attention, you come across as psychic; otherwise how would you know personal details about their life? But you really do not have to be psychic; just a little bit devious.

Like in any other serious business, you need to do some background check if you want to know the person's current status. You get to know what life is like for them in the moment and even some major occurrences that have influenced their lives so far. So when you make statements about them, statements that are factual and unique to them, it takes their breath away. It just is magical! And from then on, the person trusts you and you can read them like an open book.

Chapter 5:
Implementation of Conversational Hypnosis

Do you recall the mention that conversational hypnosis is another way of referring to covert hypnosis? Well, after outlining the scope this form of hypnosis covers, it is now time to explain how to go about the various techniques involved so that your attempts are effective and fast. Do not worry when some details come across as awkward because in time the various details you learn will make good sense when you put them together in the relevant context.

In fact, think of some complex things that you may be doing today like it is second nature, say, like driving. When learning how to drive, you are likely to have felt awkward at first with the individual moves. Coordinating the various actions from igniting the car, pressing the clutch, the accelerator and all those other moves must have made you feel as awkward as could be before an expert driver. Yet it all makes sense and comes with ease with consistent practice.

Here are helpful details pertaining to the use of covert/conversational hypnosis:

Elevated awareness
How do you tell what a person is thinking? Easy – by observing. Yes! And observing is not mere looking. You need to be intensely involved in the process; watching and sensing the feelings emanating from the person you are trying to hypnotize. You must, of necessity, register any signals the person is sending; whether it is from body language, the eyes, the breathing, everything.

That means then that your own sense of awareness must be very high in order to detect such signals. With clarity of mind and elevated awareness, you will register everything in the environment and put all the signals together instantly in a manner that helps you tell the instance the other person gets into a trance.

Repetition
In hypnosis, experts prefer to speak of hypnosis triples. In this technique, what you do is decide what you want the person you are hypnotizing to believe. Then you design statements or choose words that influence the person's thinking towards what you are saying. The more you keep repeating the statement, word or allegation the more the person is inclined to register it in the mind as reality. These hypnotic triples are just part of a wider range of persistence tactics.

Relying on the principle of successive approximations
The whole process is part of the persistence tactics we mentioned earlier. The uniqueness in this technique is that you do not insist on telling the person you are hypnotizing what you want them to believe. You just drop some point as if you are not giving it much weight and move on to other matters. Then later you mention that point again in a more elaborate manner or with more flesh. And then you let it be. Continue with your conversation in other areas and then revisit your point yet again. All these times when you are revisiting the idea you planted in the person's mind, you are intentionally developing the person's chain of thought in a certain direction.

Think of this technique as a way of communicating a big idea in a subtle manner; a way that drastically reduces the chances of overwhelm on the person you are trying to influence. In fact, on the overall, this technique is about transmitting a big idea in small doses; and of course, it makes for easier acceptability and transition for the person concerned. It ends up being a gradual creation of hallucination, where you work on the persons sense of feel, of smell, of hearing; letting the person formulate a mental picture from what you are articulating.

Applying the principle of compounding effect
This, technique, as you may well guess, has everything to do with making a greater impact on the person you are trying to hypnotize every successive time you make a move. In simple terms, once you say something to the person and the person responds positively, you need to be a little more forceful in the suggestion you bring up next. And if the person receives that suggestion with a nod too, you make the next suggestion even weightier in substance. So, the technique is about building on any success that you make in your communication with the other person.

However, in case you make a suggestion and the person you are dealing with disagrees with you or shows you an unfavorable response, you need to let that suggestion lie where it is and retrace your communication back to the point that produced success. Then proceed from that point carefully, making use of the lesson you learnt from the latest negative response. Once you resume the trend of positive response, keep building on it and you will soon have the person fully hypnotized.

Using Trance Voices
In the technique of using the trance voice, you are called upon to employ different voices when communicating to the person you are dealing with. You can vary your tone so that

sometimes you use a conversational voice while at other times you use a hypnotic voice. So at times you employ trance tonalities while other times you employ tonalities of a non-trance nature. And even during the phase when you are using trance tonalities, you are advised to be gradual and build up your communication progressively – you don't jump to use a deep trance tone at once. In fact you can look at this technique as encompassing a teaching voice; a conversational trance voice; and a hypnotic voice. And each of the voices you employ is meant to help you achieve a particular goal.

Using hot words
Use of hot words is a great technique because not only do such words stir emotions, but the emotions are of such intensity that they must show. And that is precisely what you want in hypnosis. You want to see the person's emotions because those emotions convey to you how successful you have been in influencing the person's thought process.

To be successful in hypnosis, you need to use your select hot words appropriately; in suitable context. If you, for instance, want to invoke warm feelings in someone, you could opt to use words like *love, care, trust* and such others; but you just do not use them anyhow. You must use them in an environment that is suitable; one that complements your chosen words. When thinking of the appropriate hot words to use during hypnosis, think of the words that a tabloid would use as opposed to a mainstream newspaper to convey the same message. You actually want to influence a person's thinking as strongly as a tabloid does – impacting their emotions more than their reasoning. This technique falls under the precision language of hypnosis.

Language with amplification effect
The use of amplifying language in hypnosis is also part of precision language. In this case you use words that invoke a sense of urgency in the listener. And so the person whose thought process you are trying to influence tends to respond faster than otherwise. The words you use, like instantly; *now*; *immediately*; *forthwith*; and such, dramatically work on the person's unconscious mind, making the person respond exemplary fast.

Chapter 6:
How the Hypnotic Gaze Works

This is one of those techniques that you can aptly describe as being semi-overt. It often passes as covert hypnosis, but the reality is that you do little to disguise your gaze. Instead, you direct your look towards the person you are trying to influence, maintaining direct eye contact and creating an inviting look. The hypnotic gaze, though focused, is not aggressive. It is just smooth in making the person drawn to you. So you will often find it ideal to use in everyday setting.

How do you make the hypnotic gaze effective?

This question is very valid considering that the hypnotic gaze could pass for an ordinary look from a curious person. With the gaze in this technique, you do not overpower your subject with the mental strength you are trying to impart. In fact, you wouldn't even influence their thinking with your energy. For that reason, you need to complement the hypnotic gaze with some physical mannerisms. That way, the totality of your behavior has a strong impact on the person you are trying to hypnotize.

Look at how the hypnotic gaze induction goes and the impact each move has on the person being hypnotized:

- You stand some short distance away, like an arm's length, from the person you are trying to influence as you face them directly. This way, you will be setting up the arena for the process of hypnosis.

- Look directly and steadily into the person's eyes. Let your look be anticipatory like you are curious about something the person knows. At this juncture, you are trying to unnerve the person.

- You may wish to touch the person lightly on their shoulders with outstretched hands. What you have just done is performed an action your subject did not expect.

- Now let go of the touch and lower your arms. Well, that action is a bit odd; and your subject feels as much.

- Next, open your hands and touch your subject with your palms on the upper arms just outside the shoulders. That is another unexpected action.

- Now press the person gently where you are touching them. Right there, you are beginning to cause the person curiosity.

- Repeat that press on their shoulders and say nothing. Just keep your eyes focused into theirs. That will, definitely, begin to make the person uneasy.

- Still looking at the person and retaining your comfortable hold where the hands have been for a while now, nod to yourself slightly giving the impression that something you have confirmed has given you satisfaction. That now gives the impression that you have learnt something, only the other person has no idea what it is you have learnt – call it the impact of mysterious knowledge.

- Now do another pressing of their shoulders and ensure you do it decisively; firmly with pressure. That elicits a sense of urgency in your subject.

- Next look at your subject's eyes while avoiding turning it into a stare. The best way to do that is to direct your focus on the person's nose bridge. You will be making the person feel like you are seeing right through their eyes.

- At this point, you just need to watch the person's reaction because you will have two likely alternatives: either the person will widen their eyes from fear as well as uncertainty, or the person will find himself or herself losing focus and just glazing over.

If you notice the former, do something to startle them like snapping your fingers before them. That will throw the person into a trance and then you can proceed to tell them what you feel will influence their thought process. However, if you want to play safe and not startle the person, you can simply pull them towards you gently, though firmly, and then utter the word *sleep* in a commanding tone. Those combined actions will drive the person into a trance and you can proceed to issue them with instructions on what to do next in a bid to influence their thought process.

In case what you observe is the glazing stare, just know that your subject is already in the trance stage; and you can proceed to say to them whatever you want in order to influence their thinking. However, if you are not convinced that the person is in a state of trance as yet, you can embark on swaying them gently forwards and backwards in a rocking manner as you utter the word *sleep*. Your repetitive actions and your soothing voice will get them into a trance and you can then proceed to say to them whatever you choose.

Here are some important points you need to know about hypnotic gaze induction:

Absorbing attention

Obviously, just having eye contact with someone draws the person's attention. It is inevitable. And that is what happens in the hypnotic gaze induction. If you want to draw someone into you in a powerful way, this is the technique to use. For one, it is polite to look directly into someone when speaking to them. And when someone finds you polite, they are likely to open up to you, which would help your hypnosis process a great deal.

As to how you gain the fixation attention, you actually succeed in this through a quick process that takes four stages. And in fact, to be realistic, the four stages being referred to here also help to lay the foundation for all other covert hypnosis techniques. They are the ones that fundamentally prepare your subject for hypnosis so that your subsequent moves become effective in influencing the person's thinking. It is unlikely that you could accomplish any covert hypnosis technique without the aid of these four stages. These preliminaries are, in fact, often referred to as the 4-stage protocol.

You need to realize that each of the stages involved has a technique of its own that accomplishes something unique. So, it is advisable to go through them all.

Here are those four stages:

The first stage: Absorbing attention

This is the earliest stage where the hypnosis process begins and it entails acting in such a manner as to capture the attention of your target subject. It is the point at which you get the person's attention away from everything else in the surrounding and onto whatever you are saying and also doing. As you do this, you are effectively guiding their thoughts towards a certain path of your choice.

Here are some suggestions as to how to win someone's full attention:

- Ask the person something interesting

- Tell the person something that is interesting

- Request the person to do you a favor by attending to something you need done

Of course, even in this initial stage you could still use the hypnotize gaze, which is a rather indirect method, but just know that you will need to use your best skills with this one as it is more subtle than the speaking we have just explained.

<u>The second stage: By-passing the critical factor</u>

Is it that you can only hypnotize someone who is dumb; someone who does not question things? Well, the truth is that when it comes to hypnosis, you can succeed in hypnotizing anyone as long as you know enough about human behavior and you also have the right skills to apply in your hypnosis techniques.

People are bound to wonder why they should believe what you are telling them or why they should be comfortable in your presence in the first place. That is the reason you have to be serious about this second stage of by-passing the critical factor – by-passing the querying stage.

You need to be confident that you can handle this stage well because it is very crucial in the hypnosis process. Just think about how you suggest something to a friend and the response you get is: *Forget it – been there, done that and it didn't work.* Times when you can foresee this kind of response coming, what you do is use a different approach to get your friend paying attention and taking your suggestion seriously. So you get your friend accepting your line of thought without invoking the skepticism from the logical part of her or his mind.

Therefore, get ready to sharpen the skills that allow you to bring someone on board without invoking too much reasoning on their part. If you can by-pass this critical factor, you will have a smooth ride seeing your subject taking every one of your suggestions as a welcome piece of advice; even as you know you are simply leading the person into a hypnotic trance.

The third stage: Activating unconscious response

This stage involves getting your subject responding spontaneously. What you actually want is the kind of response that someone produces when in love – one that may be illogical to an observer, but which the person gives in a matter-of-fact way. It is a response from someone under a spell. It is the kind of emotional response you want to get from your subject at this stage, and so you apply your skills of hypnosis to build great rapport with the person.

For someone to respond positively to your moves in a very unconscious way, you must have gotten them to a place of comfort and trust. And so that is what you need to work at in this stage of hypnosis.

The fourth stage: Influencing your subject's unconscious mind to your wish

This is the stage at which you begin to tell your subject of hypnosis what you would like them to believe and what you would like them to do. If the person is a salesperson, for example, and you would like them to give you a good deal in your car purchase, begin to show them a scenario in the future where they will have sold the car to you and earned a good commission on the sale. That is referred to as a future memories technique – leading the person to focus on some point in future where things are great.

In short, at this stage you use suggestion techniques to influence your subject's thought process, making them visualize an admirable outcome. Going through the above four stages successfully means you have established between you and your target subject a hypnotic interaction of a conversational nature and so you have something great to build on in your hypnotic process.

Increasing responsiveness
The reason you stare at the person you are trying to hypnotize is not because it feels good but it is only that you want to accomplish something for yourself. Otherwise staring steadily at someone can be very uncomfortable for both of you. However, it is that discomfort that gives the other person the urge to respond to you fast, having little or no room for critical thinking. Theirs at this juncture is an unconscious response – and that is good for your hypnotic process.

In fact, at this point, it actually does not matter if the response you get tallies with your motive or not. The important thing is that the person has succumbed to your provocation and said something to you. It is a start that gives you something to build your conversation on.

Suggesting a hypnotic trance to your subject
Do you realize that when you employ the hypnotic gaze induction you get yourself into some level of hypnotic trance yourself? And while at it you are effectively, though in a subtle way, communicating that state to your subject of attention. In

short, you begin by altering your own state of consciousness and then follow that with directing your subject to follow suit. And in this case, you don't need to speak out to the other person; they just feel the transmission of the message subtly happening.

Subtly communicating goodwill
In hypnotic gaze induction, just as in many other moves involving human interaction, you more or less reap what you sow. If you project hostility or unfriendliness, even without being verbal about it, you are bound to receive the same kind of response from the subject of your attention. Conversely, projecting friendliness invites friendliness. That is the reason a hypnotic gaze gets the other person responding to you positively because you pose with a friendly gesture and you use positive body language – all this in a bid to create strong rapport between you and your subject.

Exuding confidence
People listen and follow those who exude confidence. If you are to succeed while using the hypnotic gaze induction, you have got to believe that the technique is going to work and that you are going to get your subject into a trance. Avoid anything that would make you appear unsure of yourself because if you project insecurity the other person will not be eager to hear what you have got to say. Yet, as you know, interaction is the foundation of the hypnotic process.

Avoid anything that can depict you as being defensive; anything that says you can foresee the possibility of failure on your part. Such things include too much blinking; eyes that are teary; too much yawning; glancing away severally in a nervous way; portraying a rather shifty body; fidgeting; and unnerving way of talking, which is often fast and kind of mumbled.

Chapter 7:
How To Influence Emotions During Hypnosis

If you want to influence someone's emotions you have got to think about what elements are capable of triggering emotions in the person. In this process of hypnosis, look at those elements as the post-hypnotic suggestions that you give your target subject. Those suggestions, that is, those emotional triggers, are your personal creations. And so when they trigger the kind of emotions you want elicited in the other person, it is a sign that your hypnosis technique is working well.

Of course it is not just your words that are capable of triggering emotions in the other person. There is your body language to take into account as well. How you carry yourself around the person will reflect an aura of friendliness, of hostility, or mere indifference. And that in itself can trigger certain emotions in the other person. The question you need to answer yourself is if the emotions your body is setting the grounds for are the ones you wish to see at this point of interacting with your target subject.

You can even go a bit farther and use certain smells of your choice, possibly from perfumes, to make the environment more friendly or relaxing for both you and your target subject. In certain cases, you may wish to have some suitable background music in the room or whatever surrounding you are in.

Remember you want to be able to interact well with the other person, and you want to reach the person's sub-conscious with your communication. That is why all the details affecting the set-up matter. You are going to see here below the steps you need to take when using the covert hypnosis technique to ensure that you are sending emotional triggers that work.

Transmitting A Hypnotic Trigger

Remember the four-stage protocol we said earlier on is necessary as preamble for great conversational or covert hypnosis? You need to go through that with your target subject before anything else if are to be certain of a smooth hypnotic process. Just to re-cap in different words, the protocol entails:

- Absorbing the attention of your subject
- By-passing their phase of critical thinking
- Activating the subject's unconscious response
- Influencing the subject's unconscious response

Once you have successfully gone through that 4-stage phase, you have managed to set the environment for great emotional triggers.

How to effectively set emotional triggers

Follow the steps below in the order they are outlined, and you will be preparing to produce great emotional triggers for your target subject:

Clear the person's state
What exactly is that state you are clearing? Well, when you speak of your state you are normally referring to how you are in general – how you feel in terms of mood, your thought process… Generally the totality of what brings out your happiness, your discomfort, your confusion and such.

In this case, therefore, you need to do what you can to facilitate your subject have a clear mind, devoid of worries and anxieties; too much planning – just being in the now; relaxed and all perceptive to what might come along. At this stage, you are trying to create a clean slate out of your subject's mind so that they can embrace whatever you feed them on later and be able to concentrate on it.

In reality, however, it is not always easy to set someone's mind entirely clear just waiting for direction from you. Therefore what you need to strive to do is get the person in a positive mindset – being happy, relaxed, and optimistic about the future.

Identify and initiate your trigger
The trigger, remember, is that thing that gets your subject in the direction that you intend. And at this juncture when you have prepared your subject to be perceptive, your chosen trigger is bound to have a great impact. Some of the emotional triggers that work well in covert hypnosis include sounds; smells; tastes; touches; sights – things to do with your major senses.

Make an effort of conditioning the trigger
You surely aren't going to drop a trigger and divert your attention elsewhere and expect it's going to work effectively. You've got to be persistent. So, if you have chosen a particular sound as your intended emotional trigger, you need to play it and replay it, and probably replay it yet again. That is why we have spoken before of having some background music. That would be great if you have chosen the particular tune as the emotional trigger directed at your target subject.

If it is something to do with sights, depending on what you aim to achieve, you could bring out a set of photo albums; or you could enter a room ideally painted or decorated to suit your intentions. In short, whatever it is you have identified as your best trigger, let it linger around for a reasonable period of time. That way you will be getting your subject accustomed to it, and since the person is already in a perceptive state, absorbing the emotional trigger will be easy.

Testing your chosen trigger
Is your trigger working? Well, you can test that by doing a kind of re-wind, where you try and clear the mind of your target subject by, maybe, distracting them. Then you follow that move by a fresh round of trigger firing. Think about probably a situation where you abruptly switch off the nice music you had set in the background as your subject's emotional trigger. Then you immediately follow that with a serious question; probably even an academic question. Now that is a real distraction from where your subject was emotionally.

Once you set off your trigger again – the nice background music – and you cease distracting your target subject, observe and see if the emotional is working again; if it is affecting your subject in the emotional way you intend to. If it is, then you can be sure you have selected an appropriate trigger; and you can proceed with it.

Chapter 8:
How To Discharge Emotional Baggage by Self Hypnosis

And you thought it was all about other people…other target subjects? No way! You can be your own target subject; a beneficiary of your own hypnotic techniques.

The question someone might dash to ask is why you would think of taking yourself through hypnosis. Well, there is good reason for that. Sometimes you are so stressed about something from your past, or sometimes something or a combination of things that are happening in your life, that there is no better way of describing your situation than one laden with emotional baggage and psychological issues. In fact when you have lots of unresolved emotional problems, you feel like your life is on a downward spiral.

The worst bit is that in times like these you often fear that you have lost control and that there is nothing you can do about the depressing mess you are in. The question is: Is it true that you cannot reverse a personal downward emotional spiral? No, it isn't. You can clear the bad moods and emotional upheavals brought about by break-ups; frustrations; losses; and other disappointments by using hypnotic techniques.

Self hypnosis happens to be a great way for you to release pent up emotions; a way to clear your mind and get ready to embrace good news. And that should not be too difficult for you considering that hypnosis entails getting a person into a heightened level of concentration, kicking out destructive thoughts and focusing on the good ones.

Embark On Reversing Negative Thinking

The reality is that if you have ten things lined up to do, if the first one goes awry, your human weakness tells you that the other nine remaining items are likely to go just as badly if not worse. Yet there is another way of looking at the situation. You could tell yourself it's nothing to worry about really as you have nine more chances to do well. If you take the latter way of thinking, you are likely to actually do well because your mind is receptive to the goodness you are yet to see. But if you take that first way of thinking, you cannot be receptive to anything good – all you see is doom and gloom.

However, the healthy thing for you is to apply the energy you are spending on negative thinking to the opposite – positive thinking. You need to begin appreciating that you have a half-full glass – because at least you have something – and avoid looking at your glass critically as being half-empty. Thinking positively creates a healthy mental, emotional, as well as physical environment. Instead of mourning about things that have not gone right, you need to remind yourself that there is always a silver lining in the cloud. That way, you will have your eyes and mind open to identifying that glimmer of hope. Luckily, those who seek are the ones that find. And so taking yourself through a process of hypnosis is not an exercise in futility but an undertaking that can change your life drastically for the better.

Hypnotic steps you can follow to rid yourself of emotional baggage:

Stimulating hypnosis
What is it exactly you want to stimulate here? Well, you are in a bad place emotionally – that you can admit – and so you

want to stimulate your mind to be able to absorb any trace of good coming around. In fact, as long as you have decided to get emotionally healed through hypnosis, you are ready to project into your mind the bright things that can soon be.

However, you first need to ensure that your physical location and position are comfortable. Just like in meditation, you need to be in a quiet environment. You surely cannot focus on your inner thoughts and feelings when you have distracting noises all around you. In fact, you need to be within an area with least movement, if any. Then ensure that you are in comfortable wear. This book has emphasized the importance of ensuring that your target subject is comfortable as you begin your hypnotic process, and the same principle should apply to you as you carry out self hypnosis.

If your clothing is so tight you can't breathe comfortably, you can't make much headway with the self hypnosis. Any discomfort, whether physical or environmental, is an unwanted distraction. Even the environmental temperature needs to be right. Being in a warm environment is great for comfort, but you also need to guard against overdressing. Instead, dress comfortably light but have something warm around you, like a blanket, a shawl or even a sweater, which you can pick for use in case it turns chilly before you are through your hypnotic process.

And what is your best pose?

Well, that too should be comfortable. Often the recommendation is that you sit on a comfortable chair or even a couch. And if you choose to sit on a bed, that's fine too. There are some people, however, who opt to do their self hypnosis while lying down on a bed, on a couch, or even on a comfortable, very likely, carpeted, floor. Even then, that is not something this book is going to recommend with confidence unless, of course, your confidence exceeds ours, because when you lie down comfortably, you are, inevitably, susceptible to sleep. Now, is your intention to sleep off your emotional problems or get rid of them entirely? Of course the reason you want to self hypnotize is to rid yourself of accumulated emotional problems. So, get into a position of comfort, alright, but one that leaves you alert and capable of executing the moves needed in the hypnotic techniques.

As for starting off this self hypnosis, what you need to do is use the breathing techniques that you understand to help clear the negative thoughts plaguing your mind; those making you feel low and possibly lethargic. After that you can embark on using any hypnotic technique that you prefer, like eye fixation; music; or any other that you may feel comfortable applying on yourself. And since you have already gotten yourself into a relaxed state through the breathing technique, you are likely to find it easy to enter into a trance, ready to absorb positive suggestions and positive possibilities.

Visualizing Goodness
Have you realized over time how easy it is to think about negative things? Yet the unpleasant possibilities in your environment at the time may even be overwhelmingly outnumbered by the good ones. With this realization, why would you not then make a deliberate effort to focus on the possibility of good outcomes rather than dwell on the fears of unpleasant ones?

If you watch the way this discussion is going, the assertion here is that you have a choice regarding the train of thought to embrace. In this case, the process of hypnosis is very helpful.

You need to practice visualizing nice beautiful images. Think of yourself on a beautiful quiet beach, for example, watching the expanse of cool turquoise waters and enjoying the feathery feel of the breeze from the ocean. The impact of such an image is peace and tranquility; a scenic environment you never want to leave; a set-up that says to you what a beautiful world... And as you register the cool sound of the waves and feel the nice texture of the sand beneath your feet, you cannot think of a better place you be. In short, the ambience of the place, the sounds you hear; the sights you see; and everything that you feel gets you ready to accept whatever it is the world has in store for you.

Being self aware
At this stage, what you need to do is appreciate the point you are at emotionally as well as physically. Then listen carefully to your breathing. You can, obviously, tell how well you are breathing by feeling your chest rise and fall – making you know if your breathing is steady or not. You can also monitor your pulse – it could be fast, it could be mellow; but it will reflect your mental as well as physical state.

Right! You now have a pretty good idea how you feel; but you are no doctor – what do you do with that self awareness? Well, this is one unique scenario where you are going to play personal doctor. You are prepared to take yourself through the process of self hypnotization so that you can be in a better place mostly mentally. And your role at this stage is not difficult considering that you have already laid ground for the process through the first two stages. So, get on with it with confidence.

Acknowledge all the negative thoughts crossing your mind. Acknowledge too any emotional pain you are experiencing.

And also acknowledge any negative sensation that you have. Once you make that move, consolidate all that negativity and tie it up in a bundle and place it somewhere out of your way – yes, clearing the path for a positive line of thought. As you relax and prepare to imbibe the goodness of positive thoughts, the bundle of negative things you tied up will recede to the level of insignificance.

Changing your focus to brightness
What you want to do here is create some brightness in your mind. Your bundle of negativity has receded alright, but you do not want a vacuum where it left. It is therefore advisable for you to pick a color that is attractive to you and insert it in your mind so that you now have some real beauty within a radiant environment. Can surely anything go wrong in such a place? Your whole mind at this juncture is engulfed with beauty and radiance; goodness that has replaced anything dark that existed there before. You love the way you feel and you cherish what you see in your mind's eye.

Creating a way of coping
For the reason that you may have something that nagged you in the past and you never got to resolve it, flash back your mind to your most hurtful period. The consequence of that is having a flood of pain and negative emotions flushing in. Guess what you do... Well, it was a wise trap because every negative emotion that was buried is now exposed and you can easily get hold of it. With some now familiar bright light within your mind, engulf those awful feelings and crush them in. That light is too overwhelming now for those emotions you have just trapped. And they can no longer do you any harm. You have just rendered them inconsequential.

Awaken and embrace the goodness
You are now through with the self hypnosis you started, and you have nothing in your system but bright positive images and great thoughts. And you surely must be feeling good about yourself. If that is how you feel, begin to allow yourself to wake up from wonderland – remember by this time you have entered a kind of trance. Take in deep breaths and make them slow and comfortable. Repeat the breaths a couple of times until you are fully awake.

As you breathe in and out, you are, of course, absorbing the environment and becoming aware of what exists around you. Follow that with wiggling of your fingers as well as your toes in a bid to awaken your physical body from the kind of numbness that often comes with hypnotism. In fact, what you are essentially doing by wiggling your fingers and toes is facilitating energy flow right through your limbs. You can now open your eyes and enjoy the moment.

In summary, that is the process you need to take in order to free yourself of any pent up emotions; feelings that often lead to emotional instability and pain, as well as physical indisposition. Self hypnosis leaves you free of emotional baggage, happy, optimistic and confident to face the future.

Pertinent Question: *How long does self hypnosis take?*

Well, it varies from person to person; from season to season; from intensity of emotional baggage... Let's just say there is no recommended time per se. However, there are many people who speak of remaining in the trance phase for between 15min and 20min. Just have in mind when planning for the length of your session that you need to take into account the duration it takes to work your way into a trance as well as the duration it takes to get yourself out of the trance stage.

Chapter 9:
How to Hypnotize a Friend

So, obviously, you don't want to ask your friend to do something under hypnosis that would harm them or severely damage the friendship and trust you have with them. They are going to remember what they did when they were hypnotized, and they may become angry if you hypnotize them and make them do something that's unforgivable. With that fair warning, let's get started with a really fun way to hypnotize your friends.

Disclaimer: It may not work the first time or even the fifth time. It depends on the hypnotist and the person being hypnotized. So don't give up if it doesn't work the first time. Keep practicing!

Step One
First you have to find a comfortable position for both you and the person being hypnotized as the two of you could be in the same position for over half an hour. It's better that you're sitting and the person who is being hypnotized are sitting upright so that neither one of you actually fall asleep. Be sure that the person you are hypnotizing understands exactly what will happen and are willing to go through with the process.

Hypnosis is a relaxed state of mind where a person is open to suggestion. When they are in that state, they will want to please the person who is telling them what to do, but they will not do something they normally wouldn't want to do. Hypnosis is actually good for the body and mind and allows it to focus in a relaxed state. When you're hypnotized or hypnotizing someone, remember they can fall over, so be sure to be sitting down or lying down.

Step Two

If you are the one who is hypnotizing someone, be sure to speak them in a low, monotone voice. Have them stare at a picture of a spiral with a dot in the center or another object and start to tell them to look at that picture. Tell them about the picture and demand they focus on that dot in your calming, reassuring voice.

Then you want to continue to tell them to imagine how their eyelids are beginning to droop, how they are feeling calm and relaxed. Don't allow them to choose what state they are in, but demand that they are in that state. Then tell them that the next time they blink, they will keep their eyes closed and imagine that there is a spread of calm and warmth going through them. At this stage, they should be almost hypnotized, but not quite.

Step Three

In this step, you are going to repeat the second step again and ask them to open their eyes. Then ask them to blink again and leave them closed.

Step Four

Continue to address the person you are hypnotizing and keep your voice neutral and relaxing. Tell them to take five deep breaths, inhaling through their nose and holding it for a few seconds, and then out through their mouth. Each time they exhale, they'll become twice as relaxed. Tell them this. Tell them they will become more and more relaxed with each exhale, and they are feeling comfortable and warm. Then tell them how great they're doing, all in your monotone, neutral voice.

Step Five
Continue to instruct the person you are hypnotizing by telling them to relax their entire body. Then tell them to tense up the part of their body that's being worked on, and relax it. Tell them to allow the aches and pains of the day just melt away. Tell them to start with their scalp and make their way down through their body until they're at their toes. Then tell them to finish by taking a quick sweep of their body and scanning for pain and tightness. Tell them to let it all go.

Step Six
Now have them focus their attention on their right arm. Tell them to imagine that it's becoming heavy, and heavier, and heavier. With every second that passes, they can feel it sinking down. A part of them knows they can lift it if they really wanted to, but they just don't because it's too much effort and it's just too heavy.

Step Seven
Now have them focus their attention on their left arm. Imagine that arm becoming heavy, heavier, and heavier. With every second that passes, that arm feels as if it's so heavy it's sinking down. A part of them knows they can lift it if they want to, but they don't because it's too much effort and just too heavy.

Step Eight
Now have them move their focus. Tell them to focus their attention on their left leg. Imagine that leg becoming heavy, heavier, and heavier. With every second, that leg is sinking down into the floor. A part of them knows they can lift that leg if they really wanted to, but they don't because it's too much effort and it's too heavy. Now have them do the right leg. The right leg is becoming heavy, heavier, and heavier. With every second, that leg is sinking down into the floor. A part of them

knows they can lift it if they really wanted to, but they don't because it's too much effort and just too heavy. They feel as if their legs can no longer support them if they attempted to stand.

Step Nine
Now speak to the person you are hypnotizing. Tell them to picture in their mind a spiral staircase. They are standing at the top of that staircase, and they begin to walk down the stairs. With every step that they take, they feel more and more relaxed. Deeper into that state of hypnosis they go, deeper and deeper into the relaxation they sink with every step. Tell them to keep walking down, more and calmer as they keep going, down deeper into the relaxation. When they reach the end of the stairs, they will see a door, but they will not open it yet. Tell them to picture the door in their mind. Tell them to focus on its texture, color, doorknob, and hinges of the door. When they touch the doorknob, they use that signal to increase the relaxation in their body by ten times. They feel that sensation running through their body.

Step Ten
Now instruct the person to open that door and enter the room. Tell them that when they're inside, they can close the door and lock it to ensure that the journey is not going to be disturbed. Now tell them to turn and look into the room. Tell them to arrange it however they'd like. It can be full of pillows, couches, or even bean bag chairs, as long as it feels comfortable to them. Once they've done that, tell them to take a seat anywhere in the room. Tell them to take a seat anywhere that they feel comfortable and tell them they are feeling relaxed and warm.

Step Eleven
Now tell them that they are going to lift their wrist into the air, and when they do they are going to focus on their wrist. Tell them to let their wrist drop, and when it does, they will feel twice as relaxed as they did before. Tell them to do the same thing with their other wrist.

Step Twelve
Now tell them that every time they feel a tap on their back their relaxation is going to double. Tap them on the back and wait a few seconds. Tap them again in slow motions and tell them they're doing well and doing great. Continue to tap them five more times.

Step Thirteen
Now tell them that you are going to count to ten, and every time that they hear a number, they are going to become more relaxed. Count: 1, 2, 3, 4, 4, tell them they're doing well and great, 6, 7, 8, 9, 10. After you reach ten, the person should be in a deep state of hypnosis. A good way to deepen that hypnosis is to wake them up and then put them back to sleep numerous times. To wake them up, follow the next step.

Step Fourteen
When you wake up and rapidly put another person under, you will put them into a deeper state of hypnosis. Let's take a look at how you can do that first.

Tell them that when they hear the number three, they are going to be wide awake. Count to three and say 'wide awake.' Put them back to sleep using rapid induction. A common way to do this is using the eleven fingers method. Tell them to hold their hands open in front of them. Now, count their fingers, and when you get to the sixth finger, call it finger seven. They get eleven fingers then. Now give them a tug on the wrist and push them back. Say sleep suddenly when you tug on their wrist.

The person shouldn't fall, but if they do you want to catch them. Every time they are put to sleep, tell they have ten fingers and having eleven fingers is crazy. Repeat the eleven fingers trick multiple times. Now when they're in a deep state of hypnosis, have a little fun with them. You can do many things with your patient, like manipulating their sense of hearing, taste, sight, touch, and smell.

Do a little experiment with them. Tell them to act like a chicken or to pick their nose, anything that is funny and entertaining, but be sure that you don't damage the possibility of being friends with this person. Remember they will recall everything that happened to them, so don't go crazy.

Step Fifteen
In this step, you are going to wake up your patient from their hypnotic state. You want to make sure that they are asleep when you being. Tell them that they are going to be brought out of the state of hypnosis. Tell them to get up from where they are sitting and walk to the door. Tell them to unlock the door and exit the room. Then tell them to climb the spiral staircase. Tell them that with every step they are going to become more and more awake, more and more alert of their body, joints, smells, sounds and they will come out of their hypnosis. When they reach the second to last step, tell them that they will hear instructions to take the last step. They will feel refreshed, wide awake, and conscious from their hypnosis. Tell them to take that step now.

And that's it!

Chapter 10:
Instant Hypnosis

Once you have mastered the process of hypnosis that can often be called long process, you can begin to use another powerful form of hypnosis to your advantage, instant hypnosis. These techniques play with the basics of the mind and what can happen to everyone from time to time daily. Have you ever gazed out of the window and simply watched the rain come down? What about listening to music that makes you feel soothed and relaxed? Maybe watching a favorite movie or tv show and you just feel yourself tune out. Often times when this happens, you may not even notice that your brain has checked out, you're comfortable, relaxed and completely absorbed in what you are doing. It happens every day and has three characteristics that are telltale signs.

1. An increased focus and concentration.

2. Increased relaxation of the body.

3. Increased access to the subconscious mind.

Instant hypnosis simply uses this natural state of things to put your subject into that state of mind as quickly as possible.

Instant Hypnosis Technique #1

Simple, to the point suggestion
For this, powerful instant technique you simply tell the client, to sit comfortably, close their eyes and get into a state of hypnosis. This may seem a bit simplistic, but the power of suggestion is very strong and when you use a firm but modulated tone and allow the subject a small amount of time

to calm their own brain it works. As you would do for long process hypnosis, you watch for breathing and body language to assure that your subject has gone into a state of hypnosis.

Instant Hypnosis Technique #2

The handshake technique
This technique requires that you and the subject have some trust between you. As you will reach out your hand to shake with them and then pull them sharply in towards yourself, as you do this you will forcefully but calming say the word sleep. If you don't have a little trust built between you, this could just as easily backfire and make the subject tense when you pull them in. How does this technique work so easily? It works by using two separate methods of inducing hypnosis: moving the subject off balance so the brain does not have time to compute a response and giving the forceful suggestion of sleep which seems like a good idea to the brain. People are far more suggestive than they think and that is how this simple but powerful instant technique can work.

Instant Hypnosis Technique #3

Falling Backward Method
This form of instant hypnosis again works in the process of putting someone off balance and giving them a suggestion to follow. Instead of pulling them forward towards you, however, the subject will tip slightly backward. By following simple steps, this process can put your subject under in less than a minute:

Step 1: Ask your subject to stand with their feet together and their arms hanging loosely at the side. As they get into position to explain what you will be doing with them step by step so that they know what is coming next. You will let them also know this will test their relaxation reflexes.

Step 2: Move to stand directly behind your subject and place both hands on their shoulders. Stand close enough to control them as they fall, but not close enough so that they will fall directly on you. Control the fall but don't take too much weight. Place one foot in front of the other and you will be able to keep the right balance to hold their weight as they fall back. Tell the subject this is just a trial run.

Step 3: Ask your subject to relax and explain that you are going to pull them a few inches back but that you will not let them fall. Place a strong emphasis on this fact that you will not let them fall and ask them to stay relaxed and bend their body at the ankles only not at the waist, knees or anywhere else.

Step 4: With your hands still on the subject's shoulders ask them to close their eyes and pull them back only a few inches. A space of two or three inches is sufficient. Remember not to jar of force them, but allow them to gently tip backward and then rock them forward again. Keep your hands firmly on their shoulders and stand the client upright again making sure they regained their balance.

Step 5: If your subject seems relaxed move on to the next step. If not, assure the subject that they have done well, and repeat the previous step once again to make certain the subject knows what to expect. You may find that certain nervous subjects might require several attempts before they're fully comfortable.

Step 6: After having them fall back you can sit them down and use a short and brief deepening technique to make sure they are deep in hypnosis. This is usually done simply using phrases such as "move deeper and deeper into hypnosis, relax" repeat this as needed to make sure that your subject is deep into hypnosis.

The eye test

In order to confirm for both you and the subject that a state of hypnosis has been reached with an instant technique, you want to use this simple process. With your subject comfortable and sitting, follow this process:

Step 1: "You feel your eyes are very heavy and completely relaxed. Each muscle around them are now relaxed. This makes your eyelids very heavy."

Step 2: "On the count of three and not before, I will ask you to open your eyes. When I ask this, you will not be able to. You are so completely relaxed that your eyelids are too heavy. You will not be able to open your eyes because your eyelids are so heavy and you are so relaxed that you will not even try to open them."

Step 3: "Your eyelids are closed. Heavy. Sealed shut and you can't open them."

Step 4: "One. Your eyes are closed your eyelids are heavy. You can't open them not even if you try. You simply can't open them they are too heavy, so very heavy."

Step 5: "Two. You cannot open your eyes."

Step 6: "Three. Your eyes are tightly closed. Try opening them. You cannot open them right? Your eyelids are too heavy. Stop trying, just simply relax your eyes again, no more trying to open them. As go your eyes so should go your body. Relax."

Make sure when you are doing this process that you do not allow your subject to try opening their eyes for more than a second of two. If you give them too much time, they will eventually be able to force their eyes open and once they have done that they will come out of hypnosis. If they can open their eyes right away without any effort, they have not been put under and you will have to start again. If this does occur and they open their eyes simply tell them it's okay and that their eyes were not relaxed enough so you will begin again, remember to keep a positive air.

Chapter 11:
Self-Hypnosis Method

The state of self-hypnosis can be described as a state of much-focused attention with increased suggestibility. It is sometimes but not always coupled with relaxation. When someone like a therapist induces this method on someone else, it's known as hetero-hypnosis or hypnotherapy. When it's self-induced, it's called autohypnosis and is usually referred to self-hypnosis.

Self-hypnosis is usually used to modify an individual's behavior, attitudes, and emotions. For examples, numerous people use this method to help deal with everyday complications such as smoking, drinking, stress, anxiety, and depression. This method will help boost confidence and develop new skills. People who practice sports enhance their performance using self-hypnosis, and those who suffer from stress or physical pain use it to relieve their ailments.

So if you want to lose weight, quit smoking, relieve your stress or depression, or relieve physical pain, then you should try out some self-hypnosis. You can also use it in a positive manner to help you achieve your goals by suggesting to yourself that you take certain actionable steps. Self-hypnosis is powerful, so don't suggest something to yourself that you're not serious about.

Part One – Preparation

Before you even begin hypnotizing yourself, you have to prepare your state of mind and your goals for this activity. Follow these steps to get into the mood of hypnosis and to determine your goals for this exercise.

Step One

Find some comfortable clothing because it's going to be hard to enter a deep, relaxed state when you're thinking about an itchy sweater or how your jeans are too tight. Treat this as if you were going to meditate and wear some sweatpants and a t-shirt. You want nothing to distract you during this activity.

You'll also want to be sure that the temperature in the room is right, too. Have a sweater or a blanket on hand if you feel yourself getting cold, or dress in layers in case you need to take a few off to feel more comfortable. Feeling warm is going to help you feel comforted and relaxed.

Step Two

Find a quiet room and sit down in a chair that's comfortable for you, or even a couch or bed. Try not to lie down because you're more susceptible to falling asleep rather than putting yourself into a hypnotic state. Be sure not to cross your legs or your arms because you could be in this position for a long time. You don't want any part of you becoming uncomfortable.

Step Three

Be sure that you're not going to be disturbed for the following half hour. If you're interrupted by a pet, child, or a phone call, you're not going to enter a hypnotic state. Turn off all electronics, lock your door, and sequester yourself. This is time for you only.

The amount of time you want to set aside for this practice is really up to you. Most decide to be in a trance for around twenty minutes, but you also have to add the time that it will take to get ready and to recover from this hypnotic state. So half an hour is a good amount of time.

Step Four

Decide what your goals are going to be for this exercise. Do you just want to relax, self-improve, train your brain, quit smoking, lose weight, or eat better? Prepare a list of affirmations that you will lose. Self-hypnosis is just as good for relaxation as it is for those life-changing events, so many use it to a achieve goals, change thinking patterns, and give themselves some positive reinforcement and motivation. You can use some of these affirmations for your first attempt, but you should come up with your own as they're more powerful in the long run.

- Cigarettes are no longer appealing to me and I do not want to smoke.

- I am valuable and in control of my life.

- I am losing weight, eating healthy, and I feel better about life.

There are numerous different statements you can make, but be sure they are in the present tense and that you are portraying something that is already happening. Do not use statements such as: 'I will', 'I want', or 'I wish'. They do not demand that you take action now. Instead, use 'I am'.

Part Two – Entering Hypnosis

In this part, you are going to put yourself into the hypnotic state. This may take a while if this is your first time, and it could take a few tries before you get into the swing of it. So don't get frustrated if you find that you've sat there for twenty minutes and nothing feels like it's happened! You'll eventually be able to focus your mind and enter that state when you're ready.

Step One
You'll want to close your eyes and get rid of any feelings of stress, anxiety, or fear. Once you start, you might find it hard not to think about things. You might find that thoughts are intruding, and when this happens, don't try to force those thoughts to go away. Observe those thoughts with judgment and allow them to slip away on a floating cloud.

You can also pick a point on a wall and decide to focus on that point rather than close your eyes. It might be a corner, a smudge, or a dot on a piece of paper you hung on the wall. Focus on that point and concentrate on your eyelids. Repeat that they are getting heavier and heavier, and let them close when you can't keep them open any longer.

Step Two
Feel the tension in your body and acknowledge it. Begin with the toes and imagine that the tension is slowly leaving your body and going away. Imagine that each body part is being freed one at a time beginning with the toes and working all the way up to the crown of your head. Visualize every part of your body starting to become lighter when the tension leaves.

Relax your toes and feet. Continue with the legs, hips, stomach, chest, hands, arms, back, neck, and face. Use an imagery technique like water rushing over your body to get rid of all the tension.

Step Three
Now take some slow breaths and when you exhale, you can see that negativity and the tension leaving you as if it were a dark cloud. When you inhale, you can see the air is bright and filled with life and energy as it enters your body.

Now you can use visualization to relax your mind. Think about a lemon and cut that lemon in half in your mind. Imagine the juice is oozing from the lemon and flowing over your fingers. Place that lemon in your mouth. How does it taste, smell, and feel? Move on to a more meaningful vision. Imagine that your bills are taken away on the breeze, and you're running off those pounds. Get as detailed as you possibly can about what you want to accomplish. Always use the five senses of sight, sound, taste, smell, and touch.

Step Four
Now, you'll want to appreciate that you are fully relaxed. Imagine that you're at the top of a spiral staircase with ten stairs, and at the fifth step you will begin to walk into the water. Picture the details from the top to the bottom, and tell yourself that you will walk down the stairs. Count each set of steps as you go down and start at ten. Picture the numbers in your mind and imagine that every number you count the further down and closer to the bottom you get. After you count a number, you'll feel that you're drifting further into relaxation.

When you take every step, imagine the feel of the steps under the soles of your feet. Once you're at the fifth step, feel the refreshing coolness of the water and know that you're stepping into water that is pure and clean. When you begin to descend the final five steps, feel the water getting higher up your body. You should start to feel numb and your heart will race, but notice those fears and allow them to drift away.

Step Five
Now you're going to feel as if you're floating. You'll be at the bottom of the water by now and shouldn't feel anything, just the sensation that you're floating in the water. You might feel

as if you're spinning. If you don't feel this way, then try again and slower with a grasp of what's occurring. Once you've achieved the state of complete calm and relaxation, address the problems that you're having and decide what you're going to do about them.

Start to narrate what you're doing by speaking in the present and future tense quietly, or like you're reading it out of a book.

Picture there are three boxes under the water that you have to swim to. Once you've found the boxes, open them carefully and slowly, one at a time, and narrate yourself what will happen when you open the box. You might say, As I open this box, I am feeling radiance encasing me, it is becoming part of me. This light is my confidence that I will never lose because it is now part of me. Then proceed to the second box.

Avoid negative statements such as: 'I do not want to feel tired and angry'. Instead, tell yourself 'I am becoming relaxed and calm.' Use 'I am' statements.

Step Six
Repeat the statements as many times as you feel comfortable, and then feel free to wander in the water. Visualize that you're emptying the boxes and finding treasures in them, or allow the tension to flow away from you. Find areas where the water may feel hot, cold, or maybe has wildlife in it. Allow your imagination to be free.

Step Seven
At this point, you're going to begin exiting your hypnotic state. With every step that you take, you want to feel that water becoming less and less until you've reached that fifth step. When you are out of the water on the sixth step, you might

heavy or as if a weight is on your chest. Wait on that step until the feeling passes and repeat the aforementioned statements.

Once the heaviness passes, continue up the flight of steps and visualize the steps with their numbers. Feel them underneath your feet, and will yourself to go up the steps.

Step Eight
Once you've reached the top, take a few moments and breathe deeply before you open your eyes. You might want to visualize that you've reached a door and you're going to open it to get back to the outside. Do it all slowly and imagine that light is pouring in through the opening. This will make your eyes open naturally. If you have to, count down from ten and tell yourself that once you're finished, you will open your eyes.

Take your time to get up. You want to tell yourself that you are wide awake, or something that you can use to wake up. This is going to be put your mind back into a conscious state and bring you back to reality.

Please note that if you are uncomfortable with water, you will need to choose another scenario. It could be a forest, a desert, or anywhere that seems familiar, safe, and comfortable. You could even use an empty classroom. Get creative and make it something that is your own!

Part Three – Enhancement

In this step, I'm going to teach you how to make this experience really meaningful to you. It's going to be difficult enough just visualizing, but you really have to believe what is happening. So here it goes, how to enhance your experience.

Step One
First of all, you have to mean it. Mantras and self-hypnosis are not going to work and manifest themselves in reality if you don't really mean what you are saying to yourself. You have to believe in your actions and yourself in order for this to be an effective exercise. Remember, you are only limited by yourself.

If the first time is not effective, don't give up! Sometimes it takes a few tries before you get used to the experience and are good at it. Come back to the experience in a few hours or days and revisit it. You will be surprised by how much better you are the second time around.

Open your mind to the possibilities. If you're someone who is always skeptical, it's not going to work. You have to believe that there is a possibility for you to change your mindset.

Step two
There are ways that you can test yourself physically to see if you are in a trance. Some of us like to see proof that we are actually experiencing what we want to experience. You can use anything that is able to be seen or felt in your body. Try some of these ideas.

Grasp your hands together and keep them that way throughout your hypnosis. Tell yourself that they are stuck together with glue and that you cannot get them apart. Then, try to get them apart. If you can't, then you're in a trance.

You can also try to think of one arm getting progressively heavier. You don't have to actually pick one because your mind will pick one for you. Imagine that there is a book or a weight on top of it and you cannot lift up your arm. Then try to lift your arm. If you can't, then you are in a trance.

Step Three
You have to visualize. Whatever you want to work toward, like being confident, losing weight, or thinking positively, you have to visualize you're in the situation and acting like you would if you were that person. If you want to be thinner, imagine that you're putting on those skinny jeans easily, modeling in the mirror, and looking at your beautiful body. The endorphin rush is going to be worth it!

Many will use hypnosis to get rid of psychological problems like shyness. You don't have to attack this complication head on because something related will work. Just imagine that you're going about the world with your head held high, making eye contact, and smiling at those around you. This is a good first step to the more extroverted you.

Step Four
You'll want to use outside forces in order to assist you. Some people prefer to use music to get into a hypnotic state. There are many hypnosis playlists online that can help you get into the state of mind you need. If a certain scene like listening to the water or animal sounds helps you get into the mood, heave that sound at your fingertips.

Timers are also helpful as they help you get out of the trance. Sometimes it's difficult to keep track of time, and you don't want to spend hours in a hypnotic state. Just be sure that the timer has a soothing tone and isn't something jarring and frightening.

Step Five
Remember that you are using hypnosis to better yourself. You are using it to find goals that you want to achieve and concentrate on as you're relaxed. Think of who you want to be

and be that person. Hypnosis is also used for deep meditation practices, but it's better to use it for a better purpose. Many find that they come out of hypnosis with a positive mindset and a sense of purpose. Take advantage of that.

There is no wrong way to go about hypnotizing yourself. It doesn't matter if it's kicking a bad habit, focusing on your work life, or changing how you think, hypnosis is a good option. Getting rid of stress in your life is an imperative part of becoming the person you want to be, and this is going to help. And the more you practice it, the more natural it's going to become.

Tips and Tricks

There are many different ways that you can use hypnosis to help yourself. For instance, let's say that you are having trouble sleeping. Follow the countdown from ten and go down that staircase, and allow yourself to be immersed in the relaxing, pleasant state while your eyes are closed. Then lie down and sleep will find you much easier.

For those who like to meditate but are unable to sit still for a long enough amount of time, use this as a form of meditation but insert a time where you're hypnotized in between the counting down and counting up.

If you can't seem to relax your muscles properly, tense and hold them for ten seconds and then release them. This act helps you feel the tension leaving your body so that you can visualize it much easier.

Some people find that imagining a peaceful setting relaxes their mind before they count down. You can imagine that you're walking through a forest, smelling the plants and listening to the wind. You can also imagine that you're walking along the shore and you are feeling the sand underneath your feet, and the water washing your feet and ankles. You can even hear the sound of the waves.

Know what you are going to suggest to yourself before you lie down or sit down in a chair and get relaxed. Having that at your fingertips makes it much easier to remain in the hypnotic state.

Do not force yourself or to think about the hypnotic state as it will be much easier that way.

Write out the suggestions you have for yourself before you start the practice. This visual list of what you want to work on is much easier to remember than just a list in your mind.

If you find you are struggling, try to visit a hypnotherapist or purchase a recording to experience being hypnotized by someone else. Once you've experienced it first hand, you will know what you are attempting to achieve.

Now that you know how to hypnotize yourself, I suggest you practice with a timer the first few times to be sure that you don't go under for too long. It can be disorienting if you wake up two hours later when you really think it's only a few seconds, much like it is when you go under for surgery. Remember to use only positive affirmations and thought processes so that you don't instill a negative belief by accident.

Happy self-hypnotizing!

Chapter 12:
How To Tell That Someone Is In A Trance

Hey! Have we informed anyone that we are putting them into a trance? Of course not! Yet we have managed to hypnotize people – presumably – by performing some covert techniques. Now, how do you tell when you have succeeded in effectively ferrying a person into a state of trance?

This is something worth delving into because while you sometimes see signs that make it obvious someone is in a trance, other times the signs are subtle; meaning that only a trained eye will notice. However, with the right information, you will know how to tell when your subject of hypnotism has reached the trance stage.

Here are the major telltale signs:

Dilation of the pupils
When in the course of your conversation you notice the pupils of the person dilating, with the eyes looking larger than normal, it is a sign that the person is becoming relaxed in your presence. It shows that your subject has succumbed to your technique and has become comfortable with you. This simply means that you have succeeded in getting the person where you wanted them to be as far as their thought process goes.

Stabilizing of the pulse rate
How does the pulse rate come in? Well, it is known from a medical perspective that the pulse rate rises than normal when a person is unwell, upset, or overly excited. And you can tell by

having a feel of certain areas of the body where blood vessels are visually prominent – parts like the neck or the ankle.

Now, if you observe that the subject of your attention has a high pulse rate or is emotionally charged, and then you begin your process of hypnosis, you can confirm that they are getting into a trance when the blood vessels begin to relax; becoming less prominent. That is the time that the pulse rate is falling.

Stability of the breathing pattern
Just like in the case of the pulse rate, breathing is abnormally fast when a person is anxious or unwell, and it could also be abnormally slow if the person is unwell. So if you are trying to get the person to settle down by giving hypnotic assurances, then you can monitor their breathing pattern visually – but obviously, discreetly – to see how it is going. The best place to observe besides the person's chest is the shoulders. Those areas rise and fall according to the person's breathing pattern. As such you can easily tell when the breathing pattern has is regular and stabilized; and you will know then that you have succeeded in your hypnosis.

Smoothing out of the facial features
Have you any idea how a tensed up face looks like? Think of a frown, raised eyebrows or a generally contorted face. That's the look of tension right there! On the contrary, when a person is falling for your suggestions that everything is fine, you are going to notice the person relaxing. And you will know that this is going on when you see the facial lines disappearing; the contorted face smoothing out; and the symmetry of the person's face coming back to normal. In general, when you begin to look at a well balanced face, know that your covert hypnosis technique has gotten your subject into a trance.

Being deeply absorbed
There is no way a person is going to be in a trance yet keep looking from side to side – no way! When a person is in a state of trance, their eyes look steadily at one spot like they are fixated. That will tell you that their mind is engrossed in just one item or one specific thought process. At that moment, their eyes show minimal movement or none at all. And often, the eyes are glazed.

Changing of the blink reflex
Sometimes you get to know that your subject is getting into a trance by observing the changes in the blinking pattern. Sometimes the person blinks faster than before, and that becomes constant. Other times the person blinks slower, and that becomes constant too. There are even situations where the person's blinking ceases altogether. That tells you that the person's eye muscles have frozen – a state referred to as cataleptic.

Change in the manner of swallowing
In the early stages of trying your hypnotic technique on someone, you see the person having frequent swallows. Then as you get to influence the person's thinking, the swallowing mechanism tends to slow a little. That pattern progresses as you continue to succeed in your hypnosis and by the time your subject is in full trance, it is likely they will have stopped swallowing altogether. This entire change often happens in a matter of minutes.

Eyelids becoming heavy
Now, how do you know that your subject's eyelids are becoming heavy? Well, that is not so difficult to tell. The minute you notice the person looking drowsy, eyes looking all

heavy and tired, you know the trance stage has begun. It actually appears like the person is about to close their eyes.

However, if you are using one of the covert hypnosis techniques, do not anticipate the person's eyes closing because you will be in conversation with that person and they will be responding to you from time to time. In short, since in covert hypnosis the person remains consciously aware of their surroundings, they do not close their eyes; at least not completely.

Change of body movement
When you engage someone in conversation, the person usually responds verbally and also uses some body movements. If the person was particularly animated in their gestures and then you begin to notice those gestures slowing down, it is a sign that you are getting into them. Soon those gestures may disappear altogether; and you know then that you have managed to change the person's thought process; got them into a trance.

Muscles twitching involuntarily
If you see your subject of hypnosis having involuntary muscle twitches, take that as a sign that they are entering the trance stage. Often those twitches occur in the facial muscles but you can also observe them on the person's shoulders. It basically shows that the person is beginning to relax. The muscles are undergoing what can be referred to as a cathartic process.

Of course you should not take this list of signals as exhaustive. It will help for you to be observant and then you can register the changes taking place in the person you are trying to hypnotize. Some of the signs are pretty subtle and you will only notice them if you concentrate well on your hypnotic process. And mind you a person undergoing hypnotism does not necessarily manifest just a single sign – the trance stages and signals could be several. So keep an open mind and look out for as many signs as you can.

Chapter 13:
Major Mistakes To Avoid In Hypnosis

Why would mistakes occur while you are performing hypnosis yet you are the one calling the shots? Well, there are varied reasons why things go wrong even when they seem straightforward at first, but the major mistake you could make here is forgetting that you are dealing with another person who may be just as informed or as witty as you are. Of course the fact that every individual is sensitive and can tell obvious manipulation is a factor that you need to take seriously.

Of course that should not deter you from pursuing the persuasion techniques that are part and parcel of the process of hypnosis, but if there are subtle ways that you know to be effective, you had better use them to avoid making your target subject curious or suspicious of your intentions. You even need to be careful with your body language and the gestures that you use so that you can work on your subject's sub-conscious smoothly and as naturally as possible.

Here below are the major mistakes to avoid:

Shoddy Planning

If you try to carry on conversation with your subject of hypnosis the way you would with a colleague at work or the way you speak to your family at dinner time, you are bound to fail miserably. Covert hypnosis, for one, demands that you pay full attention to the person you are speaking to so that you catch all the clues that help you understand what the person's thought process is like. Now, if instead of paying full attention you are thinking about the questions to ask the person, you will lose a lot.

Again, if you don't understand the most effective words and phrases to use when conversing with a person during hypnosis, you can't get far with the process. In short, you need to prepare well for your hypnosis session whether you are doing your hypnosis formerly or otherwise.

So, to succeed in your hypnosis:

Design a favorable plan
Designing a plan of action does not mean that you make complex arrangements on how to carry on conversation with your subject. Rather, it means that you do some groundwork so that you know what generally works in trying to work someone into a trance and what doesn't work. You need, for instance, to have a good range of effective words and phrases that you can apply in communication in order to effectively write your ideas onto the person's mind.

And do not behave in stereotype when it comes to body language, your choice phrases and how you generally handle yourself when relating to that person. If you make this mistake, you may either look ridiculous or put off your subject. Yet your intention is to lure the person into trusting you so that you can both have good rapport. And although it helps better if you can get some personal details about your subject in advance, when it comes to planning for the hypnosis process, make a plan that is flexible; one that can you can use with almost anyone.

Read your subject's emotional state
Do you think you can make headway trying to hypnotize someone who is in rage or one who is suspicious of people around? It just cannot work. For one they may not even pay attention to what you are saying. That is why it is important

that you be observant and try to assess how the person is generally feeling, even before you begin your hypnosis. If you sense some tension, try and establish what is causing it. If the person is upset, find out the cause. And the reason you are trying to establish the person's emotional state is so that you can help them relax and feel at home within the environment you are in.

Remember we mentioned earlier on that you can tell that your subject is ready to get into a trance when their pause is stable and their breathing is regular. In short, a relaxed state is conducive for transitioning into a trance.

Assess the effect of your plan beforehand
You don't have to wait till you have a conversation with your subject for you to have an idea how the person is going to respond. For one, there is room to play the scene in your mind. Again you have room to assess the person's mood, demeanor and attitude as you begin to make them at ease with conversation. Something else you cannot also afford to miss includes the person's eye movements. The minute you notice your subject's eye movements begin to sway from side to side, you know time is ripe for hypnosis.

Extreme attempt at being nice

Can you personally trust a stranger who is bending over backwards to please you? Of course not! You are likely to begin questioning the person's intentions. The same thing is bound to happen to you if you show too much enthusiasm in trying to please your subject.

For you to be in a position to carry out hypnosis well on that person, you need to behave as natural as you can, and any attempt at creating rapport should flow naturally. Of course you need to be courteous as you introduce yourself and try to know the other person, but you need to guard against coming across as being too eager to please or to impress your subject. If the person becomes suspicious of you even without knowing what your intentions are, your covert hypnosis techniques will fail; and it is unlikely that other techniques will work either.

So your politeness and goodness need to reflect sincerity and a genuine attempt at helping. That way you will be able to set the stage for reading the person's mind as well as influencing their thinking.

Act desperate

First of all, appearing desperate does not attract confidence. Yet you want your target to have confidence in whatever comes out of your mouth. Actually whatever you do needs to be geared towards earning confidence from your subject, because it is that confidence that makes them receptive to what you say. And it is what you say to them that influences their thinking. And before long you'll have driven them into a trance.

So you need to guard against appearing too desperate to be in good books with your subject or too eager to be believed. Such a depiction of yourself can make your subject anxious; and an anxious person is unlikely to get relaxed to the extent of falling into a trance. And even on your part, if you become anxious you cannot be in a position to read your subject's body language well.

Be reckless with language

If you just use casual language when making conversation with your subject, do you think you are going to make an impact on their thought process? Actually, in addition to choosing your vocabulary and phrases carefully, you also need to refrain from using phrases with negative connotations. Your communication needs to be dominated by positive phrases and it needs to carry a positive tone.

Another thing is that you need to fight the temptation to talk about yourself. So avoid the use of *I*, *my* and everything else in the first person. You want your talk to be about your subject as far as possible so that you can plant some ideas in the person's mind and influence their thought process.

Be highly aggressive

Think about marketing a commodity. Have you come across those salespeople who are so aggressive in their sales attempt that they scare you away? Actually instead of making you think about the product, you end up thinking about their mannerisms and how pushy they are. Does that increase the chances of making a sale or decrease? The salesperson has put you off with undue aggressiveness, so can the chances of making a sale go any other way but down?

That is how you ruin the chances of a successful hypnosis by coming onto your subject too aggressively. Even when you want to get some information from them, be wise and subtle. You can build rapport without being too pushy or forceful. And if you are subtle and using the right words and phrases and yet you don't feel like you are making headway in getting into the person's brain, try another technique. Interrupting your process of hypnosis by altering your technique is fine; often works.

Do not deliberately lead

Look – you can't begin putting pressure on your subject to nod at what you believe should be the end result. That is bound to raise suspicion in the person's mind. Even being too serious about what you want to achieve in the end can lead you to be too direct for comfort. So, as mentioned before, proceed with the process in a subtle, kind of natural way, and before you know it your subject will be relaxed and warming up to your suggestions in a way that makes it easy for you to lead them into a trance. Keep cool, your emotions under check, and then follow the plan you have already rehearsed in your mind.

Conclusion

In conclusion, hypnosis is a real thing, but it is not what you might think it is right off the bat. It is a valid therapy and can be done quickly and easily. Like anything else, it is something that needs to be practiced. The more you use the tool, the more powerful you will become at it. It can take a little time to get used to the right phrasing and keeping your voice in a level manner however, once you master it you will be able to put anyone into a hypnotic state and help them improve their lives. Before you know it you may have friends and family begging you to use your powerful hypnosis on them for a whole myriad of things and you will be able to do it. Better still, you will be in a position to improve your own life, through self hypnosis, from one of disappointment and apathy to one of happiness and hope.

Bonus

ASTRAL PROJECTION MASTERY

Powerful Astral Projection And Astral Travel Techniques To Expand Your Consciousness Beyond The Psychical !

L. Jordan

© 2015 Copyright.

Text copyright reserved. L. Jordan

The contents of this book may not be reproduced, duplicated or transmitted without direct written permission from the author

Disclaimer : All attempts have been made by the author to provide factual and accurate content. No responsibility will be taken by the author for any damages caused by misuse of the content described in this book. The content of this book has been derived from various sources. Please consult a licensed professional before attempting any techniques outlined in this book.

Chapter 1:
What, Exactly, Is Astral Projection?

Do you know of terminologies that are not easily described in a couple of words yet you will not term them as complex as rocket science? Well, astral projection is one of them. For starters, the most direct definition of it is an out-of-body experience – commonly termed OBE. And of course, when you hear of the word *experience* you get to understand why the definition for astral projection cannot be done in a simplistic manner. Experiences can be detailed and varied even for people in the same environment.

The experience alluded to here is your and my experience – the experience of each individual when it comes to visualizing yourself from a different perspective; a viewpoint that is not ordinary as you are not in a bodily state at the time of observing yourself. In short, you are another being that you cannot touch at all, and looking at your bodily self lying down or busy doing other things. It is like you are in wonderland – remember Alice in Wonderland? So you are a liberal non-physical being, traversing wherever you want, without the inhibition of walls, doors, streams, anything physical. Now, could this be your spirit hovering about after you are dead? Oh, no, it is not! Fear not – you are still alive and breathing.

Granted, you are in a spiritual state – only you have not yet given up your physical body. Remember you can see yourself walking the earth like every other being occupying the busy rugged world. You are essentially an observer of the world you are a part of, only this time you have your double in another form – a spiritual form.

And are you sure this astral projection is not a dream? Sure, it isn't – you need to doze off to dream, something you do not need to do to get into astral projection. In fact, with the right skills, you can induce that state of astral projection at any time any place. And it is nothing like popping a sleeping pill or some tots of high alcohol concentration – just some simple consummate focusing.

Simple image of Astral Projection

Just in case you find your abstract mind getting a little muddled up with the explanation already given, let us try to crystallize the image. You have your physical body – yes that is tangibly real – and your spiritual body – that too is easy to appreciate because it is simply your subtle body. Now where you may get lost is the double existence; being in your body, yet having an out-of-body experience. And here is where we bring in the link commonly termed the umbilical cord, to get your physical and your subtle bodies to co-exist and communicate even as they part ways. Sorry, but is this like the child's umbilical cord? Well – something like that. In fact, visualize it that way for a vivid picture. However, your umbilical cord here is not made of flesh and it is not internally tying you to a fetus. It is made of energy – strong energy stream from your chakras, your physical energy points; and it is tying your physical form to your subtle form. Aha! Great – but then you have more than one chakra; more than one energy point. How does that work? Sure, that explanation is vital – you cannot afford to complicate the image that is just about to crystallize.

Luckily, you do not get to see the seven chakras in your body scramble for participation. Ordinarily, many people see this umbilical cord as coming from the navel where the conventional umbilical cord emanates from; and that is fine.

In any case, just to refresh your mind (or to inform you), the chakra at your navel is the one that contains all the energy relating to extraordinary passions like dreams and fantasies. In fact, it is said to provide a strong bond between you and people that you love. And you know in your astral projection that is usually the category of people that you get to visit. However, there is no rigidity when it comes to the location where the energy streams emanate from.

Some people see the umbilical cord as coming directly from the forehead to your subtle body. The reason you will not wish to fault this premise is that the forehead hosts the chakra in charge of imagination, intuition, and understanding of a higher force beyond our simple selves. So, yes – coming from there, the cord cannot be anything but strong in terms of helping the process of astral projection.

Anyway, just to be alive to reality, you could have your astral projection when your navel chakra is not at its strongest and the forehead chakra is just in a lull. What happens then is that your umbilical cord, which in metaphysics is dubbed the silver cord, comes directly from the chakra that is strongest at the time and links your physical body to your subtle body. Even the sacral chakra is not out of contention – you can have the silver cord coming directly from just a couple of centimeters below your navel from whence flows your sexual energy.

What you are going to realize is that once on your astral plane, everything looks and feels real – you experience things as though you were in the real world, only better. In your astral projection, you see things more broadly than you do in your earthly 220° frontal vision – yeah; you are no chameleon, remember? Yet in your astral projection, you have a whole spherical vision of 360° - at least that is the capability you have. But do you really utilize it? Sometimes no – since you are so used to looking at one direction, of course with limitation of scope, you tend to restrict yourself to that even when you are on the astral plane; and it takes practice to learn to exploit your full capability and learn to experience things comprehensively.

With practice, you get to appreciate the world without the discouragement of an aching body, an aging body or anything else physical. And what does that do to you, guess? It makes you one happy person, with a positive mindset despite any worldly challenges you may encounter. After all, astral projection brings to the fore the fact that there is a higher state of being than the physical. How encouraging!

Chapter 2:
Astral Projection Feels Like A Dream – But Is It?

Astral Projection does really feel like a dream, doesn't it? You being physically immobile and mute, yet you are seeing yourself walking or driving and chatting with people you know in real life... It does really feel like you are dreaming. But are you really in a dream state? The answer is no – dreaming is dreaming and astral projection is what it is. For one, when you are dreaming, you are on the dream plane; but when you are experiencing an astral projection, you are on the astral plane.

You see, in your mind, you have different planes, some higher and some lower than others. Each of the planes is made up of different material or content, and where the content is shared, you have different ways that the stuff is organized on the different planes. On the dream plane, for instance, you can see most of the things that you see on the astral plane. Only when it comes to organization, a dismal job shows up in your dream world. When dreaming, it is not unusual, for example, to find yourself in a ridiculous scenario where you are in a normal High school class, with your mechanic neighbor as your English teacher and the make-up of your class being two of your former elementary school classmates, one former classmate from High school, three from your university, and the rest being strangers. Surely, what can we term this but a random collection of facts and fantasy? And gladly, you know it when you are dreaming. If it was a sweet interesting dream, you wake up thinking – I wish it were true! Remember that all along, no part of you is disentangled – body or spirit.

However, when it comes to astral projection, your spiritual body leaves your physical body and ventures into deep space where there is a link between your mental contemplation and your intellect. In the discipline of theosophy as propagated by experts like Madam Blavatsky of the 1800s, the astral plane is the one that facilitates strong energy from the Prana, which is a higher plane, to seep through to your physical body. This is the exact vitalizing energy that carries you into astral travel. Essentially, you are looking at the astral plane as part of seven acknowledged planes, the lowest being the physical that is the most temporal part of your being; followed in hierarchy by the astral plane, the strong structure around which the physical body exists; and ending with the highest, which is the Atma or Pure eternal spirit.

In fact, you do not have to be deep asleep to shift to the astral plane – you can do it with full consciousness. And it is not similar to a near death experience – no. When you go through a traumatic experience, say, a serious accident, what you do is to lose consciousness and then begin to see things in a remote kind of way. In contrast, as you make your astral travel, you could still be asleep or under anesthesia, or, on the contrary, you could be fully aware of what is happening only in a kind of hypnotic trance. Surely the idea must be forming by now. And you are on the right track if you have begun to imagine having an astral projection while seated or standing in your living room or somewhere familiar for that matter. That is precisely what you are capable of achieving after you have mastered the appropriate skills of traversing the higher realms of existence.

Anything to associate astral projection with the future...?

Question: Would it excite you to know that astral projection can help you have a peek at the future?

Answer: It is actually possible for you to see beyond today through astral projection. They call it astral premonition. And you have to appreciate the import of something big or serious happening when you have prior knowledge of it. Whether it be something good or bad, it does help you to take it in when you have been psychologically prepared than if it catches you unawares. Or have you not heard of people collapsing after receiving overwhelmingly good news just as others collapse of bad news? In any case, who would not like to be forewarned if only to satisfy some curiosity?

Reasons you and others would be interested in astral projection:

- That much talked about curiosity that killed the cat

  You want to experiment and see if you can actually master astral projection, and if so, how far you can go with it. Fair enough – curiosity is part of human nature.

- To interact with other astral beings like spirits of loved ones who are departed

- To allow your physical body to relax

  As you are aware, as long as there is activity of any kind within you, spiritual or otherwise, it will take some energy from your body. As such, any chance for relaxation is more than welcome

- To get some information from that extraordinary spiritual world

- To try and understand the after-life in a better way

- To achieve some healing by releasing any negative energies and tapping into the positive ones.

And just in case it has not yet dawned on you, astral experiences are related to the stars – those bright celestial bodies that bring light and energy into your life, both physical and spiritual. So, no – when you are having a starry projection, you are not dreaming. You are trying to make a brighter life for yourself.

CPSIA information can be obtained
at www.ICGtesting.com
Printed in the USA
FSOW02n2054040816
23466FS